MW01199093

the day-by-day method

Writing Chinese with Ease

The Characters stroke-by-stroke

by
Philippe Kantor

adapted for English-speakers by **Clare Perkins**

ASSIMIL

B.P. 25
94431 Chennevières-sur-Marne Cedex
FRANCE

ISBN : 2-7005-0295-7

 **Method**

Other Assimil titles available in handy book format with cassettes and CDs

"With Ease" series
Arabic with Ease
Armenian with Ease*
Chinese with Ease vol. 1
Chinese with Ease vol. 2
Writing Chinese with Ease
Dutch with Ease
German with Ease
Hungarian with Ease
Italian with Ease
Japanese with Ease vol. 1
Japanese with Ease vol. 2
Writing Japanese with Ease
New French with Ease
Spanish with Ease

For travelling
Dutch from the Word Go!
French from the Word Go!
German from the Word Go!

Advanced language skills
Using French
Using Spanish

"Business"
Business French

For children
Sing your way to French!

* Available soon

CONTENTS

Example of jīnwén calligraphy by Yolaine Escande.

The aim of this book is to initiate the beginner in the art of writing Chinese, using the 800 most common characters of modern Chinese.

Their introduction follows the progression of the 105 lessons of *Chinese with Ease* but it is also possible to use this book independently. In order to satisfy the needs of the greatest number of students, the explanations can also be followed by those who do not necessarily wish to learn to speak Chinese.

We hope that the explanations in the introduction, the list of radicals and the appendices will provide you with the material for acquiring a sound basic knowledge of Chinese writing, of the best aesthetic quality! Enjoy your study!

At the end of the volume, the bilingual *Index of characters* will refer you to the lesson where each character is introduced. This **character index** supplements the **word index** at the end of Volumes One and Two of *Chinese with Ease*. Taken together, they form a basic Chinese-English dictionary.

Eight examples of calligraphy of the character 东 dōng by Yolaine Escande.

PRESENTATION

This method for **learning to write** the characters will help you to complete your study of the Chinese language; the object of volumes 1 and 2 of *Chinese with Ease* being spoken Chinese. Each character is presented stroke by stroke, and all the basic characters introduced during the 105 lessons have been analysed in this way.

Before beginning the exercises, it is a good idea to read the *Introduction to Writing* again (pages xviii to xxiv in volume 1), as a reminder of the basic rules of Chinese writing.

At each stage in your apprenticeship, you must devote a certain amount of time to the memorization of the new characters. The best way to do this is to use the age-old method of "lines": on calligraphy paper with large squares, copy each character at least ten times, or more if you find it hard to remember, until you can easily write it from memory. At the end of each lesson, test yourself on it and on the preceding lessons, to make sure that you remember all the characters and that you can write them all with the strokes in the right order.

If you have forgotten the meaning of a character, you can refer to the corresponding lesson, where it was introduced for the first time.

For each lesson, only the **new** characters are analysed stroke by stroke. You may find that one of the characters in a word or an expression has already been studied in combination with other characters, with a different meaning. In that case, the stroke by stroke analysis is not repeated. You can refer to the *index* to find the lesson number where the character first appeared.

A good way to test your progress is to check that you know the meaning of each character, that you can pronounce it correctly and that you can use it in a bisyllabic word or in an expression or sentence from the corresponding dialogue.

You will not find any lessons numbered with multiples of seven (7, 14, 21, etc.). These are the revision lessons in *Chinese with Ease*, they refer to the six previous lessons and do not include any new characters.

CHINESE WRITING

x •

BASIC STROKES

The basic strokes of Chinese writing can be divided into eight groups:

STROKE		EXAMPLES
dot	、	法 雨 汉 六 书
horizontal	一	一 二 三 工 于 天
vertical	丨	十 五 干 工 上 下
rising	ノ	法 我 北 地
left curve	丿	人 入 六 文 八 大 刀
right curve	乀	人 入 六 文 八 大 长
hook	一 亅 乚 乀 亅 乚	你 小 民 我 象 儿
double hook	勹 乁 勹 乛 了 乁	马 飞 力 及 字 说

• Horizontal strokes are always written from left to right, and vertical strokes from top to bottom.

• Be careful of the rising stroke: it is only distinguished from the left curve by the direction in which it is written. These strokes can be combined to form composite strokes.

So a vertical stroke | joined to a horizontal stroke ⟶ gives ∟ as in 山 shān. A horizontal stroke ⟶ and a left curve ノ gives ㇆, as in 汉 hàn etc.

The most usual combinations of strokes are:

horizontal + vertical	⟶ + | = ㇇
vertical + horizontal	| + ⟶ = ∟
horizontal + left curve	⟶ + ノ = ㇆
left curve + rising stroke	ノ + ╱ = ∠
rising stroke + vertical + hook	╱ + ㇚ = ㇙
left curve + right curve	ノ + ╲ = く

Exercises

Write a line of each of the basic strokes in the squares below. When you have filled them in, use your own similar squared paper to repeat the exercise five or six times.

THE EIGHT RULES
OF CHINESE WRITING

Calligraphy is a complete art form in itself, and is closely related to painting and poetry. However, it is necessary to understand the basic rules of structure, line and balance, because they determine harmony, stability and aesthetics.

Each character in the same text should be contained in the same sized imaginary square. Some characters only have one or two strokes, and others twenty or more. So each stroke must be given the right dimension so that when the character is completed, whatever the number of strokes, it fits into the imaginary square. And it should be as harmonious as possible, respecting the rules of balance and stability. The character must not lean either too far to the left nor too far to the right. Its composition must respect the proportions of each element. Characters containing many strokes will have each element reduced in size so that the size and balance of the completed character is respected.

On the other hand, characters with few strokes should occupy the space in the imaginary square as fully as possible.

The strokes should not be drawn mechanically. A stroke, the horizontal stroke for example, can be drawn in many different ways, according to its length or its position within the character. The left curve and the right curve should descend far enough to provide a balanced base for the character.

Although respecting these basic notions will not necessarily lead to "beautiful" calligraphy, they will help you to write **correctly**, so that your characters are both **legible** and **pleasant** to read.

Mastery of the art of calligraphy is only acquired after several years of training. More than any other, Chinese writing allows the expression of one's personality and one's feelings as one prepares to put brush to paper.

Movement, rhythm, balance or passion can all be expressed in a text, a poem or even in one single character when the calligraphy is by an expert hand. (See illustration p. vi)

At your level, using a fairly hard fine-point felt-tip pen, try to train yourself to write clearly and carefully in order to acquire a sound foundation in Chinese writing, your springboard from which to embark on a serious study of calligraphy.

You can also refer to Lin Si Chen's *Elementary Chinese Calligraphy* (published by Sino-thai), a short English language guide to beginners' calligraphy which is a good introduction to this age-old art.

The basic rules for the order of strokes when writing a Chinese character are as follows:

1. Horizontal strokes are written before vertical strokes, except when the horizontal stroke is the last stroke at the bottom of a character.
2. Left curves are written before right curves.
3. Upper elements are written before lower elements.
4. Elements on the left come before those on the right of the character.
5. An outer element is written before filling in.
6. Certain "tripod" characters are written in the following order: middle, then left side, then right side.
7. Surrounding elements are prepared with two strokes and then filled in before being closed.
8. When it is situated on top and to the right, a dot is written last.

These rules are reviewed again in the following chart, with examples provided.

Writing rules

EXAMPLES

THE CHARACTER   IS WRITTEN

1. horizontal then vertical

十   一 十

天   一 二 干 天

2. left curve then right curve

八   丿 八

文   亠 亠 文

3. from top to bottom

豆   一 豆 豆 豆

兰   丷 兰 兰 兰

4. from left to right

明   日 明

地   圡 地

5. from outer to inner

问   门 问

风   几 风

6. middle, left then right

小   亅 小 小

木   一 十 才 木

7. fill in the surround
before closing

国   丨 冂 国 国

回   丨 冂 回 回

8. dot written last

书   乛 马 书 书

发   一 夂 发 发

• xvii

According to the composition of the character and the lay-out of its different elements, you can refer to the appropriate rule. By practising you will find that the rules of stroke order eventually become automatic.

Here are some of the possible compositions using different elements to make up a character, and their position relative to each other:

LAY-OUT OF THE DIFFERENT ELEMENTS IN A CHARACTER

lay-out	冂	吕	回	冂	匚	吕	冂	冂
example	他	音	国	则	区	想	筷	懂

GRAPHICS AND PRESENTATION

In China, rough paper is usually printed with squares. Each character takes up a square, as does each punctuation mark. At the beginning of each new paragraph two squares should be left empty.

A full stop is written using a little circle.

Nowadays, most texts are written horizontally, from left to right. However some books or articles, certain letters or poems are still written in the "old style", that is vertically, starting on the right hand side of the page and filling in towards the left, column by column. Newspapers still use both styles, providing journalists with a varied and lively style of presentation

Importance of Precision when Writing

Some characters are very similar. They may only differ by one small stroke. They may have the same number of strokes and only differ in the way they are set out. You must be very careful to respect the lay-out of the strokes and their position in relation to each other. Be careful to position the beginning and end of each stroke correctly. Be careful not to cross or intersect strokes that should not meet, or you may be writing a completely different character with a completely different meaning!

Look at the following characters, which are similar in composition:

EXAMPLES OF CHARACTERS WITH SIMILAR STROKES

大	big	太	too much	天	heaven
干	to do	千	thousand	十	ten
八	eight	人	man	入	to enter
边	side	力	strength	刀	knife
小	small	少	few		
早	early	旱	drought		
住	to reside	往	towards	佳	good
白	white	百	hundred		
木	wood	本	root	不	not

RADICALS

The radical is the symbolic element giving an indication of the semantic family to which a character belongs. Knowing the radical of a character helps with memorization. Radicals are also the means for "spelling" a character .

For example 李 lǐ (*plum*) is 木 + 子 = 李, mù+zǐ=lǐ: lǐ is made up of mù (*wood*) and zǐ (*child*).

访 fǎng is fāng with the *word* radical 讠, etc.

Each radical has its own place in the composition of a character. It is not necessarily the same for each of the 214 radicals.

The *hand* 扌, *word* 讠, *clothing* 衤 are usually on the left side of the character.

The *roof* 宀, *grass* 艹, *claw* 爫 are at the top of the character.

The *knife* 刂 is on the right side of the character. The *heart* 忄 is at the bottom of the character, etc.

Others like *earth* 土, may either be at the top, at the bottom or on the left side of the character!

In order to recognize the different elements that make up the characters you meet in the lessons, refer to the *Table of Radicals* at the end of this book.

In Chinese dictionaries, the characters are generally listed by their radical, but as there are often more than one hundred characters with the same radical, another element is also used to classify each character. Usually it is the number of strokes that make up the rest of the character.

So 说 shuō (*to speak*) is listed with the *word* radical 讠, with the characters of more than 7 strokes.

The character 国 guó (*country*) has the *surrounding wall* radical 囗, and is listed with the characters with more than 5 strokes.

If you are aware of all these elements and their position in the character you will find it easier to consult a Chinese dictionary. This is one of the reasons why you should pay careful attention to the radicals, the basic strokes and their order.

THE DIFFERENT STYLES OF WRITING

Since their first primitive pictographic forms, Chinese characters have been evolving constantly up to the present day modifications and simplifications.

In the brief summary of different styles of writing the most important are:

• The jiǎgǔwén script on bones or tortoiseshells from between 1400 and 1150 BC. This is the earliest known form of Chinese script.
• The jīnwén script engraved on bronze objects dating from the Zhou dynasty, 1122 to 255 BC.

• The 专书 zhuànshū or sigillate script, still in use today to engrave seals.
• The lìshū official or chancellery style script dating from the Qin dynasty (3rd century BC). This script already makes greater use of straight lines.
• The kǎishū or regular style, which was developed in the 3rd century AD.

The kǎishū style is still in use in China today. It is used for teaching in schools and forms the basis of the different scripts used in printing.

In 1956, in continental China characters were simplified. Many had the number of their strokes reduced. Some radicals were also simplified.

This form of writing is used most widely today: it is used in *Chinese with Ease.*

In Taiwan, among overseas Chinese, and also to a great extent in Hong Kong, the non-simplified script is still used. For those who

The Evolution of Chinese Writing

Different Styles

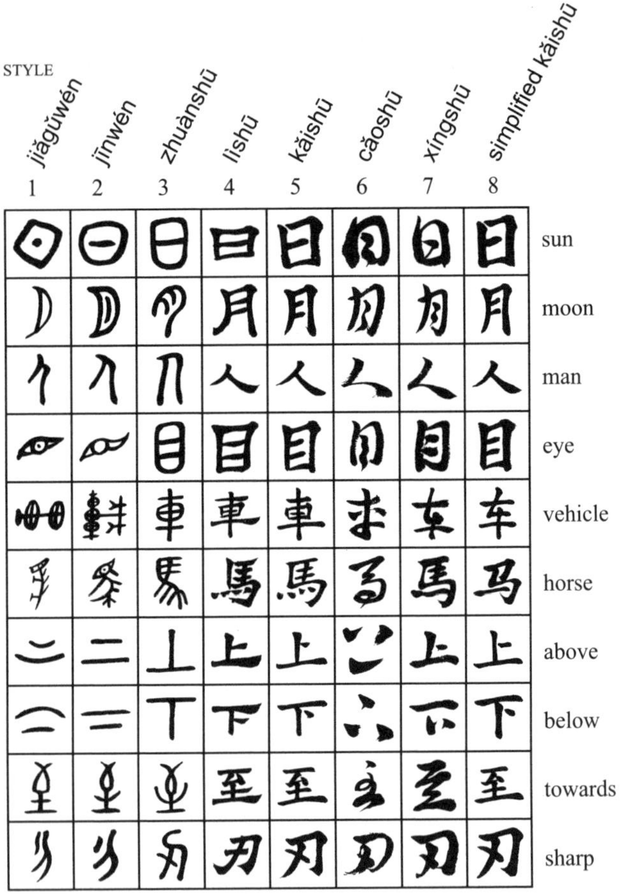
STYLE
1 jiǎgǔwén
2 jīnwén
3 zhuànshū
4 lìshū
5 kǎishū
6 cǎoshū
7 xíngshū
8 simplified kǎishū
sun
moon
man
eye
vehicle
horse
above
below
towards
sharp

wish to learn the earlier system, the non-simplified characters are also given at the end of each line.

When they write quickly, the Chinese adopt a more concise style, the xíngshū, or cursive script where certain strokes are joined up in order to keep the brush or pen in contact with the paper as much as possible. The cǎoshū script is even more fluid and is used on certain occasions (taking notes, writing letters, composing poetry, etc.). It is sometimes very difficult to decipher, even for the Chinese reader.

Models

In the following section you will find all the characters introduced during the 105 lessons in *Chinese with Ease*. They are presented lesson by lesson, by order of appearance.

The models are presented stoke by stroke, in the order for writing. As well as the phonetic transcription and the meaning of the character in isolation, its radical is indicated so that you know to which "family" the character belongs and how it is classified in a dictionary.

The non-simplified versions of characters are also given. These are still in use in Hong Kong and in Taiwan.

Remember

If no new characters are introduced in a lesson, then that lesson is not included in this volume.

How to Work

Take a sheet of squared paper and using a fine felt-tip or ballpoint pen, copy each character several times stroke by stroke, being careful to respect the order. Copy or, if you wish, trace the models. Then copy out each character at least ten times, *reading it out loud* at the same time. This is the best way to memorize Chinese, fixing in your memory both the **sound** (pronunciation) and the **gesture** (stroke by stroke, in the correct order).

On page xxvii you will find an example of the sort of squared paper that Chinese schoolchildren use for doing their "lines" of writing.

Do not hesitate to work in the same way. Repetition is an effective memory aid. And it works for spoken Chinese, as you see in the lessons in *Chinese with Ease*, or for written Chinese, as you are about to find out!

Advice

When you have finished studying the characters for a certain lesson, go back to the corresponding lesson in *Chinese with Ease* and learn to read the dialogue in Chinese, without referring to the phonetic transcription.

Make yourself a card for this purpose. Cut out horizontal strips so that when you place the card on the left-hand pages of *Chinese with Ease*, only the lines of dialogue in characters are apparent. In this way you can easily test yourself and hear how your reading is progressing.

Preliminary exercise

Write a line of each of the following basic strokes:

丶							
一							
丨							
丿							
丿							
㇏							
→							
㇚							
大							
小							

人							
你							
女							
子							
口							
不							

EXERCISES

We advise you, for each of the following lessons, to copy each new character five or six times, stroke by stroke, then to copy the whole character at least ten times. Use calligraphy paper or paper with big squares and a fine-point pen.

WRITING PAPER MODEL FOR EXERCISES

1   First Lesson

	PINYIN	MEANING	RADICAL	MEANING
你	nǐ	you	亻	person
好	hǎo	good, well	女	woman
饿	è	hungry	饣	food
吗	ma	(*interrogative*)	口	mouth
我	wǒ	I	戈	axe
不	bù	not, no	一	one
累	lèi	tired	田	field
走	zǒu	to leave	走	walk

Note. When the character is one that was simplified in the 1956 writing reform, the *complex form* is also given at the end of the line, in grey tint.

丿 亻 亻 亇 竹 你 你

く 女 女 幻 奵 好

丿 亇 亇 钅 钅 饣 饣 饿

饿 饿　　　　　　　　　　　餓

丨 冂 日 叮 吗 吗

一 一 干 手 我 我

一 丆 不 不

丨 冂 月 冊 田 畧 畧 畧

畧 累 累

一 十 土 圥 耂 走 走

These are still in use in Hong Kong, Taiwan and in overseas Chinese community publications.

第	dì	number		⺮	bamboo
一	yī	one	一		horizontal
课	kè	lesson	讠		word
练	liàn	} exercise	纟		silk
习	xí		冫		ice
完	wán	finish	宀		roof
成	chéng	to become	戈		spear
句	jù	sentence	口		mouth
子	zi	*(suffix)*	子		son, child

Note. Be careful not to confuse the ice radical 冫 (two drops of water) with the water radical 氵 (three drops)!

丿 ⺮ ⺮ ⺮ ⺮ 笁 筈 笒

笃 筜 第

一

丶 讠 订 识 诇 诇 诇 课

课课 　課

乙 纟 纟 纟 纤 练 练 练 練

刁 习 习 習

丶 丷 宀 宀 宀 宇 完

一 厂 厃 成 成 成

丿 勹 勺 句 句

乛 了 子

2 Second Lesson

要	yào	to want	女		woman
饭	fàn	food, cooked rice	饣		food
汤	tāng	soup	氵		water
菜	cài	vegetables, dish	艹		grass

什	shén		亻		person
么	me	which? what?	丿		curve
面	miàn	flour, noodles	一		one

包	bāo	parcel	勹		to wrap
二	èr	two	一		one

一 厂 厂 丙 两 两 西 要 要 要

丿 𠂉 𠂉 𠂉 饣 饣 饭 饭　　飯

丶 丶 氵 氵 汚 汤 汤　　湯

一 十 艹 艹 茓 茓 芯 茊

苹 莱 菜

丿 亻 仁 什　　甚

丿 厶 么　　麼

一 亅 厂 厂 币 而 而 面 面

　　麵

丿 勹 勹 匀 包

一 二

Note. For the water radical, be careful to write the third stroke the right way: it is a rising stroke!

3 Third Lesson

买	mǎi	to buy	大		big
书	shū	book	丨		vertical
笔	bǐ	brush, pen	⺮		bamboo
报	bào	newspaper	扌		hand
也	yě	also	丨		vertical
那	nà	so	阝		ear
裤	kù	trousers	衤		clothing
三	sān	three	一		one

Advice. For 那 make sure to write the two horizontal strokes before intersecting them in the middle.

一 亠 亇 亖 买 买　　買

乛 九 书 书　　書

丿 𠂉 𠂊 𠂋 𠂌 竹 竺 竺

竺 笔　　筆

一 亅 扌 扌 扌 报 报　　報

乛 力 也

丁 刁 刁 刁 那 那 那

丶 丶 衤 衤 衤 衤 衤 衤

衤 裤 裤 裤　　褲

一 二 三

For 书 be careful to keep the character symmetrical, the vertical stroke should cross the horizontal elements in the middle. The lower horizontal element should be larger than the upper one.

4 Fourth Lesson

他	tā	he	亻		person
是	shì	to be	日		sun
谁	shéi shuí	who?	讠		word
父	fù	father	父		paternal
亲	qīn	parent	立		stand
哦	ò ó	oh!	口		mouth
就	jiù	so, then	亠		lid
呀	ya	ah!	口		mouth

丿 亻 仃 仲 他

丨 冂 冃 日 旦 旱 旱 昰 是

丶 讠 讠 讠 诅 讠 诈 诈
诈 谁　　　　　　　誰

丿 八 分 父

丶 亠 亠 立 立 辛 辛 亲
　　　　　　　　親

丨 冂 叮 口 叮 叮 吁 吁 哦
哦 哦

丶 亠 广 亣 古 亨 亨 京
京 就 就 就

丨 冂 口 叮 呀 呀 呀

认	rèn	to know	讠	word
识	shí	to know	讠	word
见	jiàn	to see	见	see
过	guo	(*experiential suffix*)	辶	walk
四	sì	four	囗	surrounding wall

5 Fifth Lesson

这	zhè, zhèi	this, that	辶	walk
儿	r	(*suffix*)	儿	son
有	yǒu	to have	月	flesh
没	méi	to not have	氵	water
画	huà	drawing	一	horizontal

丶 讠 订 认 认 認

丶 讠 订 讱 讱 识 识 識

丨 冂 贝 见 見

一 才 寸 寸 讨 过 過

丨 冂 冂 四 四

Note. For this form of the *walk* radical, strokes 2 and 3 are usually connected and written as a single stroke.

丶 亠 疒 文 文 讠文 这 這

丿 儿 兒

一 ナ 才 右 右 有

丶 冫 氵 氵' 沪 汐 没 没

一 丁 厂 冃 丙 面 画 画 畫

店	diàn	shop, store	广		shelter
邮	yóu	postal	阝		ear
局	jú	office	尸		corpse
对	duì	exact	寸		inch
起	qǐ	to stand up, to get up	走		walk
五	wǔ	five	一		horizontal

Note. The meaning given here is for each character in isolation. However, when a character is used with other characters to form a

6 Sixth Lesson

老	lǎo	old	耂		old
李	lǐ	plum	木		wood
王	wáng	king	王		king

丶 亠 广 庐 庐 庐 店 店

丨 冂 日 曲 曲 邮 邮 　郵

フ ヨ 尸 局 局 局 局

フ ヌ ヌ 对 对 　　對

一 十 土 丰 丰 丰 走 起

起 起

一 丁 五 五

word, the meaning may be fairly different from the meaning of each character taken separately.

一 十 土 耂 耂 老

一 十 才 木 李 李 李

一 二 干 王

| 在 | zài | to be at | 土 | earth |
| 六 | liù | six | 、 | dot |

8 Eighth Lesson

去	qù	to go	土	earth
吃	chī	to eat	口	mouth
太	tài	too	大	big
想	xiǎng	to think	心	heart
行	xíng	satisfactory	彳	to walk
七	qī	seven	一	one
八	bā	eight	八	eight

Note. There are several *walk* radicals: 彳 辶 走.

一 ナ 才 存 存 在

丶 亠 六 六

一 十 土 去 去

丨 冂 口 叮 吒 吃

一 ナ 大 太

一 十 才 木 朩 相 相 相 相

相 相 想 想 想

丿 夕 彳 彳 行 行

一 七

丿 八

Be careful not to confuse 彳 and 亻, the *person* radical!

9 Ninth Lesson

住	zhù	to reside	亻		person
房	fáng	house	户		house
安	ān	peace	宀		roof
静	jìng	calm	勹		wrap
很	hěn	very	彳		walk
爱	ài	to love	爫		claw
人	rén	men, people	人		person
幸	xìng	} happily	十		ten
亏	kuī		一		one
九	jiǔ	nine	丿		curve

丿 亻 亻 亻 亻 住 住

丶 亠 宀 户 户 户 户 房

丶 丷 宀 宀 安 安

一 二 丰 丰 丰 青 青 青

青 青 青 静 静 静　　**静**

丿 ノ 亻 行 行 行 很 很 很

一 爫 爫 爫 爫 严 严 孚

爱 爱　　　　　　　　**愛**

丿 人

一 十 土 土 寺 击 击 幸

一 二 亏　　　　　　　**虧**

丿 九

10   Tenth Lesson

冷	lěng	cold	冫	ice
出	chū	to go out	丨	vertical
哪	nǎ	where?	口	mouth
新	xīn	new	斤	pound
晚	wǎn	late, evening	日	sun
十	shí	ten	十	ten

11   Eleventh Lesson

她	tā	she	女	woman
妹	mèi	younger sister	女	woman
朋	péng	} friend	月	flesh
友	yǒu		又	again

、 冫 冫 冫 冫 冷 冷

乚 凵 屮 出 出

丨 冂 日 叮 叮 叼 哵 哪 哪

、 亠 立 立 辛 辛

亲 亲 新 新 新

丨 冂 日 日 旷 旷 旷 晄 晚 晚 晚

一 十

乚 女 女 如 如 她

乚 女 女 妦 妠 妹 妹 妹

丿 几 月 月 月 朋 朋 朋

一 ナ 方 友

中	zhōng	middle		丨		vertical
国	guó	country		囗		surrounding wall
当	dāng	} of course		小		small
然	rán			灬		fire

们	men	(*plural*)		亻		person
孩	hái	child		子		son
几	jǐ	how many?		几		how many
知	zhī	} to know		矢		arrow
道	dào			辶		walk

Note. There are two variants of the *fire* radical. On the left, it is 火. Below, it is four dots 灬. The first stroke is written towards the left, and the other three towards the right.

丨 冂 口 中

丨 冂 冂 冃 甲 国 国 国 國

丶 丷 严 当 当 當

丿 ク 夕 夕 夕 夕 夕 状 状

状 然 然 然

丿 亻 亻 们 们 們

了 了 子 子 孑 孑 孩 孩 孩

丿 几 幾

丿 一 一 与 矢 矢 知 知 知

丶 丷 丷 丷 产 首 首 首

首 首 道 道

12   Twelfth Lesson

颜	yán	color	页	leaf
色	sè		勹	to wrap
喜	xǐ	to like	士	scholar
欢	huān		欠	debt
漂	piào	pretty	氵	water
亮	liàng		亠	lid
吧	ba	(*suggestion particle*)	口	mouth
贵	guì	dear, expensive	贝	shell, cowrie

Note. Be careful not to confuse the *scholar* radical 士, with 土, the *earth* radical. In the *scholar* radical the upper horizontal stroke is longer than the lower horizontal stroke. In the *earth* radical, it's the contrary.

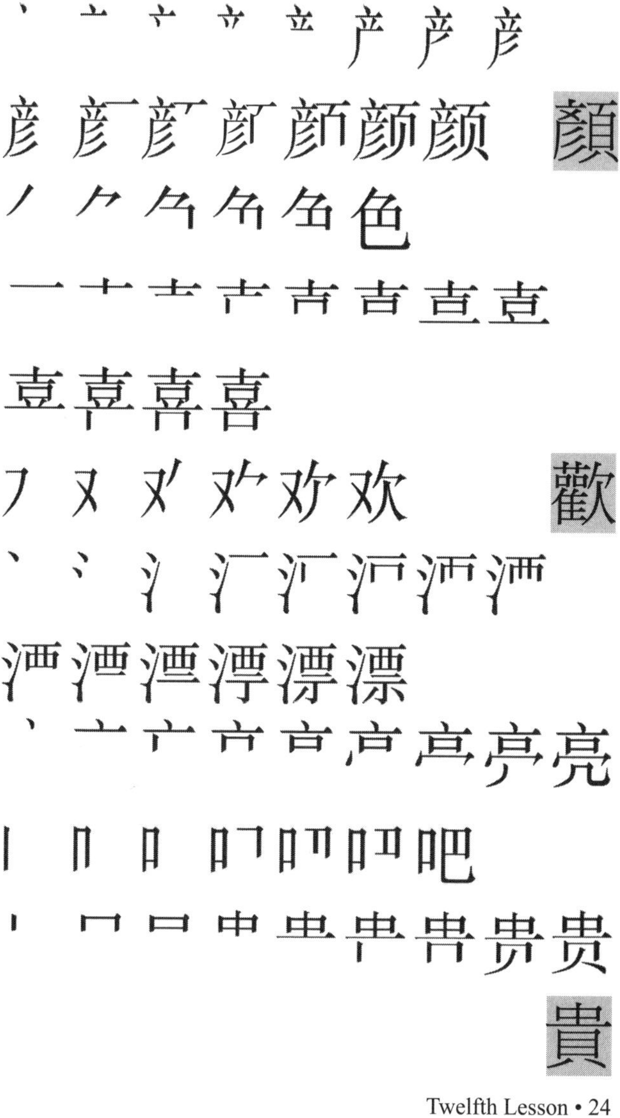

颜 顏
色
喜
欢 歡
漂
亮
吧
贵 貴

可	kě	but	一		one
大	dà	big	大		big
的	de	(*particle*)	白		white
怎	zěn	how?	心		heart
办	bàn	to do	、		dot
小	xiǎo	small	小		small

13 Thirteenth Lesson

| 做 | zuò | to do, to make | 亻 | person |

翻	fān			羽	feathers
		translate		
译	yì			讠	word

一 丁 兀 可 可

一 ナ 大

＇ 亻 亻 白 白 白 的 的

＇ 二 亇 仟 乍 乍 怎 怎 怎

フ 力 办 办　　　　　辦

亅 小 小

丿 亻 什 什 什 估 估 做 做

做 做 做

一 二 三 平 平 平 来 来 来

番 番 番 番 翻 翻 翻 翻 翻

＇ 讠 订 译 译 译 译　　譯

会	huì	to know	人	person
英	yīng	English, brilliant	艹	grass
语	yǔ	language	讠	word
点	diǎn	little, few	灬	fire
呢	ne	(*particle*)	口	mouth
说	shuō	to speak	讠	word
写	xiě	to write	冖	cover
文	wén	language	文	language

Note. Be careful not to confuse *cover* and *roof* radicals: 冖 and 宀.

丿 八 公 公 会 会   會

一 艹 艹 艹 芦 芎 英 英

丶 讠 汀 讥 诺 语 语 语 语   語

丨 ├ ┝ 占 占 卢 占 点 点   點

丨 冂 日 旷 旷 旷 旷 呢

丶 讠 讠 讠 说 说 说 说   說

丶 宀 写 写 写 写   寫

丶 亠 方 文

There are two variants for *to do*, zuò: 做 is usually used for practical movements, whereas 作 zuò is more likely to be for abstractions.

15   Fifteenth Lesson

明	míng	light, clear	日	sun
回	huí	return	口	surrounding wall
家	jiā	family, home	宀	roof
远	yuǎn	far	辶	walk
车	chē	vehicle	车	vehicle
开	kāi	to open, to drive	一	one
骑	qí	to mount, to ride	马	horse
自	zì	self	自	self

Note. In *home*, under the family roof 宀, you will find 豕: a *pig*!

丨 冂 冂 日 日 明 明 明

丨 冂 冂 冋 同 回

丶 宀 宀 宀 宁 宁 家 家
家 家

一 二 テ 元 元 远 远　遠

一 ナ 左 车　　　　　　車

一 二 于 开　　　　　　開

乛 马 马 驭 驴 驴 骄 骄
骄 骄 骑　　　　　　　騎

丶 丆 冇 白 自 自

16   Sixteenth Lesson

票	piào	ticket		西	west
快	kuài	fast		忄	heart
里	lǐ	in		里	li, distance measurement
等	děng	to wait		竹	bamboo
火	huǒ	fire		火	fire
半	bàn	half		丨	vertical
还	hái	again, still		辶	walk
时	shí			日	sun
间	jiān	time		门	door

Note. There are two forms of the *heart* radical. Below, it is 心. On the left, it is 忄.

一 厂 厅 币 両 両 西 亜

票 票 票

丨 亅 忄 忄 忙 快 快

丨 冂 月 日 旦 甲 里　　裏

丿 𠂉 𠂤 𥫗 𥫗 竹 竺 竺

竿 笁 等 等

丶 丷 少 火

丶 丷 半 半 半

一 丆 オ 不 不 还 还　　還

丨 冂 月 日 旷 时 时　　時

丶 亍 门 门 问 间 间　　間

It can be written 忄 or 忄, according to habit or style of script.

多	duō	many	夕		eve
块	kuài	currency unit	土		earth
钱	qián	money, cash	钅		metal, gold
够	gòu	enough	夕		eve
了	le	(*particle*)	亅		vertical hook

17 Seventeenth Lesson

下	xià	below, down	一		one
象	xiàng	like	豕		pig

Note. 象 in other contexts also means *elephant*.

ノ ク タ 夕 多 多

一 十 土 圵 圵 块 块　　塊

丿 𠂉 𠂆 𠂊 钅 钅 钅 钱

钱 钱　　　　　　　　錢

丿 勹 勺 句 句 够 够 够

够 够 够

乛 了

一 丁 下

丿 𠂊 𠂉 负 负 负 争 象

象 象 象

雨	yǔ	rain	雨	rain
公	gōng	public	八	eight
园	yuán	garden	口	surrounding wall
意	yì	} meaning	心	heart
思	si		心	heart
事	shì	affair	丿	vertical hook
待	dāi	to remain	彳	walk

Note. 意 is sometimes simplified as 忥.

---

18 Eighteenth Lesson

| 马 | mǎ | horse | 马 | horse |
| 师 | shī | master | 巾 | cloth |

一 厂 厅 帀 帀 雨 雨 雨

丿 八 公 公

丨 冂 冂 冃 冃 园 园　　園

丶 亠 亠 立 产 音 音

音 音 意 意 意

丨 冂 月 用 田 田 思 思 思

一 厂 丆 丏 写 写 事

丿 丿 彳 彳 犷 徉 待 待 待

⁊ 马 马　　馬

丨 丿 丬 扩 师 师　　師

姐	jiě	elder sister	女	woman
候	hòu	time, wait	亻	person
来	lái	to come	一	one
清	qīng	clear, transparent	氵	water
楚	chǔ	clear	疋	fabric
告	gào	} to warn, to inform	口	mouth
诉	su		讠	speech
看	kàn	to see	目	eye

Note. For 清, there is an unofficial simplification: 氵青.

姐　　候　　来　　清　　楚　　告　　诉 訴　　看

病	bìng	illness	疒		illness
您	nín	you (*polite*)	心		heart
舒	shū		舌		tongue
		at ease, comfortable			
服	fu		月		flesh
姓	xìng	to be called	女		woman
叫	jiào	to call	口		mouth
宝	bǎo	treasure	宀		roof
定	dìng	sure	宀		roof

丶 亠 广 广 疒 疒 疒 病
病 病
丿 亻 亻 伖 你 你 你 你
您 您 您
丿 人 卜 卢 全 全 舍 舍
舍 舒 舒 舒
丿 刀 月 月 肝 胐 服 服
く 夕 女 女 妒 妒 姓 姓
丨 口 日 叩 叫
丶 丷 宀 宀 宀 宇 宝 宝 寶
丶 丷 宀 宀 宁 宁 宇 定

19 Nineteenth Lesson

怕	pà	to fear	忄		heart
路	lù	road	𧾷		foot
次	cì	time	冫		ice
能	néng	to be able	月		flesh
最	zuì	most	日		sun
打	dǎ	to strike	扌		hand
听	tīng	to listen	口		mouth

Note. Recent dictionaries no longer make the distinction between radical 74 月 (*moon*) and radical 130 月 (*flesh*).

41 • Nineteenth Lesson

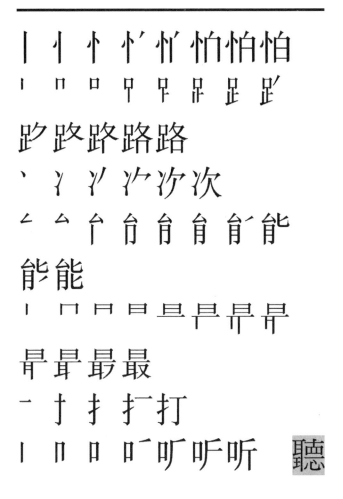

丨 丨 忄 忄 忄́ 忄́ 怕 怕 怕

丨 冂 口 吊 吊 吊 趵 趵

趵 跠 跠 路 路

丶 丷 丷 汀 汻 次

厶 厶 匀 匀 匀 匀 匀́ 能

能 能

丨 冂 冂 日 日 旦 旱 旱 旱

旱 旱 最 最

一 丁 扌 扩 打

丨 冂 冂 口 口́ 叮 听 听 聽

Remark. The unsimplified character for *to listen* had the *ear* radical 耳. The simplified character now has the *mouth* radical 口!

20   Twentieth Lesson

两	liǎng	two	一		one
男	nán	masculine, male	力		strength
女	nǚ	feminine, female	女		woman
现	xiàn	current	王		king
岁	suì	year of age	山		mountain
忘	wàng	to forget	心		heart
真	zhēn	true	十		ten
算	suàn	to count	⺮		bamboo
问	wèn	to ask	口		mouth

Note. 男 nán, *masculine*, may be written in two different ways. Either *sun-strength*, in which the left curve of *strength* crosses the *sun*: 日 + 力; or *field-strength*: *field* is written first and then underneath *strength* is written separately 田 + 力.

一 丁 丁 丂 丙 两 两

丨 冂 日 田 田 甲 男

く 女 女

一 二 于 王 王 珏 玕 现 現

丨 屮 山 屮 岁 岁 歲

丶 亠 亡 亡 忘 忘 忘

一 十 广 古 古 肖 直 真 真

丿 𠂉 𥫗 𥫗 𥫗 𥫗 竺 竺

笁 筲 筲 筲 算 算 祘 問

丶 冂 门 门 问 问

Note. In most dictionaries, for certain characters where the radical is difficult to identify, a loose system of classification is adopted: these characters appear under several possible radicals. So for 岁, *year of age*, it may be found under 夕 (*eve*), or under 山 (*mountain*).

22 Twenty-second Lesson

热	rè	hot	灬	fire
情	qíng	feelings	忄	heart
以	yǐ	} before	人	person
前	qián		刂	blade
刚	gāng	just	刂	blade
迎	yíng	to welcome	辶	walk
学	xué	to study	子	son
化	huā	to spend	亻	person
极	jí	very	木	wood

一 十 扌 扌 执 执 执 热

热 热 热　　　　　　　　热

丨 忄 忄 忄 忄 忄 情 情

情 情 情

乚 以 以 以

、 丷 丷 产 产 前 前 前 前

丨 冂 冈 冈 刚 刚　　　　刚

丿 丨 口 卬 卬 迎 迎

、 丷 丷 丷 丷 学 学 学 學

丿 亻 亻 化

一 十 才 木 朴 朳 极 极 極

毕	bì	to finish	十	ten
业	yè	domain	业	domain
专	zhuān	specially	一	one
历	lì	} history	厂	cliff
史	shǐ		口	mouth

23 Twenty-third Lesson

奇	qí	} strange	大	big
怪	guài		忄	heart
抽	chōu	to pull	扌	hand
枝	zhī	(*classifier*)	木	wood
谢	xiè	thanks	讠	word

一 匕 比 比 比 毕　　　**畢**

丨 刂 业 业 业　　　**業**

一 二 专 专 专　　　**專**

一 厂 厅 历　　　**歷**

丨 口 口 史 史

一 ナ 大 太 존 奇 奇 奇

丨 忄 忄 忄 怪 怪 怪 怪

一 扌 扌 扣 扣 扣 抽 抽

一 十 才 木 杧 杧 枝 枝

丶 讠 讠 讠 讠 讠 讠 讠

讠 讠 谢 谢　　　**謝**

烟	yān	smoke	火		fire
筷	kuài	chopsticks	竹		bamboo
用	yòng	to use	用		use
啊	a	ah! (*exclamation*)	口		mouth
才	cái	only	一		horizontal

24 Twenty-fourth Lesson

进	jìn	to enter	辶		walk
城	chéng	town	土		earth

丶 丷 少 火 灯 灯 炬 烟

烟 烟 煙

丿 ⺮ 竹 竹 笁 竺 竿 竿

筲 竿 竿 筷 筷

丿 几 月 月 用

丨 冂 口 吖 吥 啊 啊 啊

啊 啊

亠 寸 才

─ 二 丰 井 丼 讲 进 進

一 十 土 圢 圹 圻 城 城

城

礼	lǐ		衤	rites
拜	bài	} week	丿	curve
跟	gēn	with, to follow	⻊	foot
到	dào	towards	刂	blade
南	nán	south	十	ten
京	jīng	capital	亠	lid
商	shāng	commerce	亠	lid
都	dōu	all	阝	ear
各	gè	each	口	mouth

、 ﹀ ㇏ 礻 礻 礼　　　　　　禮

一 ＝ 三 手 手 手 手 拜 拜

丨 冂 口 甲 甲 甲 足 足

足 足 跙 跙 跟

一 乛 云 云 至 至 到 到

一 十 广 古 市 两 南 南 南

、 ㇒ 亠 ㅜ 宁 京 京

、 亠 亠 亠 广 肖 肖

商 商 商

一 十 土 耂 耂 者 者 者

者 都

ノ ク 夂 各 各 各

种	zhǒng	sort, type	禾		grain, cereal
百	bǎi	hundred	一		one
货	huò	merchandise	贝		shell, cowrie
馆	guǎn	hall	饣		food
接	jiē	receive	扌		hand

Note. In ancient times, cowrie shells were used as currency.

---

25   Twenty-fifth Lesson

门	mén	door	门		door
长	cháng	long	丿		curve
概	gài	general, approximate	木		wood

一 二 千 禾 禾 和 和 和 种 種

一 一 丆 丆 百 百 百

丿 亻 亻 化 化 华 货 货 貨

丿 丷 乍 乍 乍 乍 馆 馆 馆
馆 馆 馆 館

一 十 扌 扩 扩 扩 护 护 护
接 接 接

丶 宀 门 門

丿 一 长 长 長

一 十 才 木 机 机 机 根
根 柑 柑 概 概

午	wǔ	midday	丿	curve
请	qǐng	to invite	讠	word
先	xiān	firstly	丿	curve
上	shàng	to ascend	一	one
共	gòng	together	八	eight
汽	qì	steam	氵	water
坐	zuò	to sit	土	earth
站	zhàn	station	立	stand
口	kǒu	mouth	口	mouth

Note. For 请 there is also the simplification 请.

丿 ⺈ 𠂉 午

丶 讠 讠 订 请 请 请 请

请 请　　　　　　　請

丿 ⺈ 牛 生 牛 先

丨 卜 上

一 十 廿 廾 共 共

丶 丶 氵 氵 汽 汽 汽　　汽

丿 人 𠆢 从 丛 坐 坐

丶 亠 六 方 立 立 立 站 站

站 站

丨 冂 口

后	hòu	after	厂		shelter
再	zài	then, again	一		one
换	huàn	to change	扌		hand
反	fǎn	reverse	又		again
正	zhèng	right, correct	止		stop

26 Twenty-sixth Lesson

决	jué	to decide	冫		ice
俩	liǎ	two people	亻		person
结	jié	to tie	纟		silk

一 厂 厂 斤 后 后　　　後

一 丁 厅 厅 再 再

一 十 扌 扩 护 护 换 挽
换 换

一 厂 厉 反

一 丁 下 īF 正

丶 冫 冫 沪 决 决

丿 亻 仃 仃 行 俩 俩 俩 俩
俩

乙 乡 纟 纟 纤 纤 结 结 结 结
結

婚	hūn	marriage	女	woman
张	Zhāng	(name)	弓	bow
红	hóng	red	纟	silk
月	yuè	month	月	moon
昨	zuó	yesterday	日	sun

27 Twenty-seventh Lesson

北	běi	north	匕	spoon
陈	Chén	(name)	阝	ear
生	shēng	to bear, to be born	生	born
已	yǐ	already	已	already

Note. Be careful! 已 yǐ is only half closed. It is neither 巳 sì nor 己 jǐ!

く　タ　女　女ノ　女ノ　女ノ　姃　姃

姃　婎　婚

フ　フ　弓　引ノ　弘ノ　张　张　　張

ㄥ　ㄥ　纟　纟　红　红　红　　红

丿　刀　月　月

丨　刀　冃　日　日ノ　旷　旷　昨　昨

丨　十　土　圤ノ　北

マ　阝　阡　阼　阵　陟　陈　　陳

丿　广　仁　牛　生

フ　ヨ　已

经	jīng	to pass	纟	silk
教	jiāo	to teach	攵	letters
肯	kěn	to accept	止	stop
法	fǎ	law	氵	water
为	wèi	for	丶	dot
因	yīn	because	囗	surrounding wall
得	de	(*particle*)	彳	walk

29 Twenty-ninth Lesson

| 旅 | lǚ | tourism | 方 | square |

幺 幺 幺 纟 纟 纟 纟 经 **經**

一 十 土 耂 耂 孝 孝 教

教 教 教

丨 ト 止 屮 肯 肯 肯 肯

丶 冫 氵 汇 汁 泮 法 法

丶 ソ 为 为 　　　　**爲**

丨 冂 冋 冈 因 因

丿 彳 彳 彳 彳 彳 彳 得

得 得 得

─────────────────────

丶 亠 方 方 方 方 方 旅

旅 旅

错	cuò	error	钅	metal
水	shuǐ	water	水	water
己	jǐ	self	己	self
今	jīn	today	人	person

---

30 Thirtieth Lesson

喝	hē	to drink	口	mouth
渴	kě	to be thirsty	氵	water
茶	chá	tea	艹	grass
近	jìn	near	辶	walk

丿 ｆ ⺒ ⺒ 钅 钅一 钅十 钅䒑

钅丗 错 错 错 错　　　　錯

亅 刀 水 水

㇇ ㇕ 己

丿 入 仒 今

―――――――――――――

丨 冂 冂 冂𠃊 冂冂 冂冃 冃冃 曷

喝 喝 喝 喝

丶 丶 氵 氵 沪 浔 浔 浔

渴 渴 渴 渴

一 十 艹 芍 艻 茐 芩 茶 茶

一 厂 厂 斤 斤 近 近

| 忙 | máng | busy | 忄 | heart |
| 班 | bān | organization | 王 | king |

---

31 Thirty-first Lesson

该	gāi	duty	讠	word
桥	qiáo	bridge	木	wood
牌	pái	card	片	slice

---

32 Thirty-second Lesson

| 地 | dì | earth | 土 | earth |
| 方 | fāng | square | 方 | square |

丨 忄 忄 忙 忙 忙

一 二 干 王 王 玎 玑 玗
班 班

丶 讠 讠 讠 讠 该 该 该 **該**
一 十 才 木 杧 杁 杤 杴
桥 桥 　　　　　　**橋**
丿 丿 尸 尸 片 片 牌 牌
牌 牌 牌 牌 牌

一 十 土 圢 圽 地
丶 亠 宀 方

重	chóng	again		里		*li,* distance measurement
庆	qìng	festival		广		shelter
年	nián	year		丿		curve
觉	jué	to find		见		see

卖	mài	to sell		十		ten
东	dōng	east		一		one
工	gōng	work		工		work
厂	chǎng	factory		厂		cliff
海	hǎi	sea		氵		water

Remember. Do not confuse 买 mǎi, *to buy* and 卖 mài, *to sell*. The only difference: the cross on mài.

一 二 干 干 言 言 言 重 重 **重**

、 亠 广 庁 庄 庆 **慶**

丿 仁 仨 仨 甠 年

、 丷 丷 丷 兴 兴 兴 岢 觉

覺

一 十 吉 吉 吉 吉 卖 卖 **賣**

一 左 左 东 东 **東**

一 丁 工

一 厂 **廠**

、 丶 氵 氵 氵 汇 汇 海 海

海 海

33 Thirty-third Lesson

难	nán	difficult	又		again
话	huà	word	讠		word
字	zì	character	宀		roof
比	bǐ	compared to	匕		spoon
较	jiào, jiǎo	relatively	车		vehicle
容	róng		宀		roof
		easy			
易	yì		日		sun
花	huā	flower, to spend	艹		grass
录	lù	to record	水		water

ヮ ヌ ヌ ﾈ ﾈ ﾈ 잣 难

难 难　　　　　　　難

丶 讠 讠 讠 讠 讠 话 话　話

丶 丷 宀 宀 宁 字

一 上 上 比

一 宇 车 车 车 车 车 车

轫 较　　　　　　　較

丶 丷 宀 宀 宍 突 突 容

容 容

丨 冂 日 日 日 尹 尹 易 易

一 十 艹 艹 艹 花 花

フ ヨ ヨ 寻 寻 寻 录 录　錄

音	yīn	pronunciation	日	sun
机	jī	machine	木	wood
广	guǎng	vast	广	shelter
和	hé	and	禾	grains, cereals
懂	dǒng	to understand	忄	heart

34 Thirty-fourth Lesson

| 复 | fù | again, repeat | 夂 | follow |

36 Thirty-sixth Lesson

信	xìn	letter	亻	person
给	gěi	for	纟	silk
封	fēng	to seal	寸	thumb

丶 亠 产 产 产 音 音 音

一 十 才 木 杉 机 機

丶 亠 广 廣

一 二 千 禾 禾 利 和 和

｜ 忄 忄 忙 忙 忙 忙 懂

懂 懂 懂 懂 懂 懂 懂

╭ ┌ ┌ 乍 亡 复 复 復

丿 亻 亻 亻 信 信 信 信 信

乚 乚 纟 纟 纱 纱 给 给 給

一 十 土 圭 圭 圭 圭 封 封

妈	mā	mother	女		woman
另	lìng	other	力		strength
放	fàng	to put down, to place	攵		letters
假	jià	holiday	亻		person

早	zǎo	early	日		sun
同	tóng	together	冂		limit
板	bǎn	plank, board	木		wood

Advice. If you now start learning the meaning of characters in isolation, you will find it easier, later on, to understand the meaning of certain words that include those characters. For example 同 tóng (*together*,

---

37　Thirty-seventh Lesson

讲	jiǎng	to explain, to tell	讠 word

く　女　女　妇　妈　妈　　　　媽

丨　冂　口　马　另

丶　亠　广　方　方　扩　放　放

丿　亻　伫　伫　伫　佢　佢　伫
佢　假　假

丨　冂　月　日　旦　早

丨　冂　冂　同　同　同

一　十　才　木　札　杤　板　板

in unison, same), is part of the expressions 同年 tóng nián (*to be born the same year*); 同意 tóngyì (*to be of the same opinion, to agree*); 同学 tóngxué (*classmate*); 同志 tóngzhì (*comrade*), etc.

丶　讠　讠　讠　讲　讲

亿	yì	hundred million	亻	person
止	zhǐ	to stop	止	stop
题	tí	problem	页	leaf
杂	zá	complicated	木	wood
藏	zàng	Tibetan	艹	grass
内	nèi	internal	冂	limit
蒙	měng	Mongolian	艹	grass
言	yán	language	言	language

丿 亻 亿　　　　　　　　　　億

丨 卜 止 止

丨 冂 日 日 旦 早 早 是 是

是 是 题 题 题　　　　　题

丿 九 九 杂 杂 杂　　　雜

一 十 艹 艹 芹 萨 萨 萨

萨 萨 萨 萨 萨 萨 藏 藏

藏 藏

丨 冂 内 内

一 十 艹 艹 芦 芦 营 梦

梦 蒙 蒙 蒙 蒙

丶 亠 亠 言 言 言 言

| 州 | zhōu | district | 川 | river |

---

38 Thirty-eighth Lesson

飞	fēi	to fly	乙	2nd of ten heavenly stems
场	chǎng	field, terrain	土	earth
非	fēi	not (be) } very	丨	vertical
常	cháng	often }	巾	cloth

高	gāo	high } pleased	亠	lid
兴	xìng	happy }	八	eight
位	wèi	(*classifier*)	亻	person

Note. Be careful not to confuse 兴 xìng and 光 guāng.

丶 丿 ⺀ 少 州 州 州

乁 飞 飞　　飛

一 十 土 圹 场 场　　場

丨 十 十 丰 非 非 非 非

丷 丷 丷 丷 兴 兴 兴 兴

兴 兴 常

丶 亠 广 亠 言 户 高 高

高 高

丶 丷 丷 兴 兴 兴　　興

丿 亻 亻 广 伫 位 位

授	shòu	to give	扌	hand
介	jiè	} to introduce	八	eight
绍	shào, shao		纟	silk
原	yuán	origin	厂	cliff
谅	liàng	to pardon	讠	word
关	guān	} to close } contact	八	eight
系	xì	} relation	纟	silk
如	rú	as, like	女	woman
果	guǒ	fruit	木	wood

79 • Thirty-eighth Lesson

一 十 扌 扩 扩 扩 扩 扩
扩 拧 授
丿 人 介 介
ㄥ ㄥ ㄠ ㄠ 纟 纫 纫 绍 绍 **绍**
一 厂 厂 厂 厉 厉 厉 原
原 原
丶 讠 讠 讠 讠 讠 讠 讠
讠 谅   **諒**
丶 丷 丷 兰 关 关   **關**
一 乙 乙 玄 系 系 系   **係**
ㄑ 女 女 如 如 如
丨 冂 冂 冃 旦 甲 果 果

慢	màn	slow	忄	heart
零	líng	zero	雨	rain
況	kuàng	situation	冫	ice
只	zhǐ	only	八	eight
熟	shóu, shú	ripe, cooked	灬	fire
悉	xī	familiar	心	heart
司	sī	services	亅	hook

Note. Zero is sometimes written ◯ . It is written slightly larger in proportion to other characters than the Roman numeral 0.

丨 忄 忄 忄 忄 忄 悍 悍

悍 悍 悍 悍 慢 慢

一 广 户 币 币 币 币 币

币 币 币 零 零

丶 丬 氵 沪 沪 沪 况

丨 冂 口 只 只 祇

丶 亠 广 亠 亩 亨 享

享 孰 孰 孰 孰 熟 熟

一 丆 平 平 平 采 采

悉 悉 悉

丁 丬 司 司 司

| 带 | dài | to carry | 巾 | cloth |

---

39 Thirty-ninth Lesson

| 电 | diàn | electricity | 日 | sun |
| 喂 | wèi | hallo! (on the phone) | 口 | mouth |

找	zhǎo	to seek	扌	hand
志	zhì	will, aspiration	心	heart
久	jiǔ	long time	丿	curve
谈	tán	to discuss	讠	word

| 空 | kòng | free time | 宀 | roof |

一 十 卅 卅 卅 卅 带 带 带

带

一

｜ 冂 冃 日 电

電

｜ 冂 冃 冄 冂冂 冂冂 冂甲 冂甲

喂 喂 喂 喂

一 ナ 扌 扩 找 找

一 十 士 吉 志 志 志

丿 ク 久

丶 讠 讠 订 沙 谈 谈 谈

谈 谈

談

丶 丷 宀 宀 宂 空 空 空

麻	má	hemp	广		shelter
烦	fán	bothered	火		fire
饺	jiǎo	dumplings	饣		food

40 Fortieth Lesson

参	cān	to visit	厶		cocoon
观	guān	to see	见		to see
研	yán	} research	石		stone
究	jiū		宀		roof
所	suǒ	place, office	斤		axe
立	lì	to erect	立		stand

丶 亠 广 广 庁 庂 床 庲
麻 麻 麻

丶 ⺍ ⺌ 少 火 灯 灯 灯 炳
炳 炳　　　　　　　　煩

丿 丷 饣 饣 饣 饣 饣 饣 饺 饺　餃

ㄥ 厶 厺 乡 矣 矣 参 参　參
㇇ 又 㣎 㣎 观 观　　　　　觀
二 厂 石 石 石 矿 矿 研
丶 丷 宀 宀 宀 穷 究
一 厂 斤 斤 斤 所 所 所
丶 亠 亠 立 立

主	zhǔ	principal	丶	dot
搞	gǎo	to do	扌	hand
脑	nǎo	brain	月	flesh
网	wǎng	web	网	net
产	chǎn	production	立	stand
由	yóu	by	田	field
单	dān	single	八	eight
负	fù	to carry on one's back	贝	shell, cowrie
责	zé	responsible	贝	shell, cowrie
无	wú	not have	一	one
线	xiàn	thread	纟	silk

、 亠 亠 主 主
一 十 扌 扩 扩 扩 护 护
护 搞 搞 搞 搞
丿 刀 月 月 𦝠 肪 肪 肪 脑
丨 冂 冂 冈 网 网
、 亠 产 立 产 产　　　産
丨 冂 曰 由 由
、 丷 丷 丷 肖 肖 单 单　單
丿 𠂉 个 负 负 负　　　負
一 一 丰 丰 青 青 责 责　責
一 一 于 无　　　　　　無
乚 纟 纟 纟 纟 线 线 线　線

41　Forty-first Lesson

演	yǎn	to act	氵	water
排	pái	row, line	扌	hand
戏	xì	theatre	戈	spear
者	zhě	he who	耂	old
舍	shè	house	人	person
死	sǐ	dead	一	one
世	shì	world	一	one
惜	xī	to regret	忄	heart
休	xiū	to rest	亻	person

丶 冫 氵 氵 氵 沪 沪 沪
沪 泸 泮 漙 演 演
一 十 扌 扌 扐 扐 扐 排
排 排 排
乛 又 又 戏 戏 戏 　　戲
一 十 土 耂 耂 者 者 者
丿 人 仌 仐 全 仐 舍 舍
一 厂 歹 歹 歹 死
一 十 廿 廿 世
丨 忄 忄 忄 忄 忄 惜 惜
惜 惜 惜
丿 亻 仁 什 休 休

| 息 | xī | to rest | 心 | heart |
| 份 | fèn | (*classifier*) | 亻 | person |

43 Forty-third Lesson

满	mǎn	full	氵	water
哥	gē	elder brother	一	one
收	shōu	to receive	攵	whip
活	huó	alive	氵	water
惯	guàn	accustomed	忄	heart
胖	pàng	fat	月	flesh

′ ⼍ ⼞ 自 自 自 自 息 息 息

丿 亻 ⼴ 仂 份 份

丶 丶 氵 汇 汇 汁 汁 汁

浩 浩 满 满 满　　　滿

一 丆 帀 帀 哥 哥 哥 哥

哥 哥

ㄥ ㇄ ㇆ 屮 屮 收 收

丶 丶 氵 汇 汇 汗 汗 活 活

丨 忄 忄 忄 忄 忄 惯 惯

惯 惯 惯　　　慣

丿 刀 月 月 月 肦 肦 胖 胖

香	xiāng	scented	日		sun
港	gǎng	harbor	氵		water

---

44 Forty-fourth Lesson

猪	zhū	pig	犭		animal
肉	ròu	meat	肉		meat
毛	máo	hair, fur	毛		hair
斤	jīn	pound (weight)	斤		axe
别	bié	other	刂		knife
肠	chǎng	entrails	月		meat

Remember. For 毛 the first stroke is *the left curve*, the next two are *horizontals*.

一 二 千 禾 禾 禾 香 香 香

丶 冫 氵 氵 氵 氵 氵 洪

洪 洪 港 港

丿 亅 犭 犭 犭 狞 狞 狞

猪 猪 猪

丨 冂 内 内 肉 肉

一 三 三 毛

一 厂 斤 斤

丨 冂 口 号 另 别 别

丿 刀 月 月 肜 肜 肠 肠 腸

| 特 | tè | special | 牛 | ox |
| 少 | shǎo | little | 小 | small |

45 Forty-fifth Lesson

外	wài	outside	卜	divination
边	biān	side	辶	walk
春	chūn	spring	日	sun
本	běn	root	木	tree
感	gǎn	to feel	心	heart

| 冒 | mào | to risk | 日 | sun |
| 让 | ràng | to let, to give way | 讠 | word |

丿 ㇒ 牛 牛 牜 牛 牜 牜 特 特 特

丨 ㇚ 小 少

丿 ㄅ 夕 列 外

㇆ 力 力 边 边　　　　　　　邊

一 二 三 声 夫 夫 春 春 春

一 十 才 木 本

一 厂 厂 厂 厉 咸 咸 咸

咸 咸 感 感 感

丨 冂 冂 冃 冃 冐 冒 冒 冒

丶 讠 计 计 让　　　　　　　讓

需	xū	to need, to want, to require	雨	rain
实	shí	real	宀	roof
借	jiè	to borrow, to lend	亻	person
应	yīng	should, ought to	广	shelter

47 Forty-seventh Lesson

属	shǔ	to belong	尸	corpse
爸	bà	father	父	paternal
牛	niú	ox	牛	ox
动	dòng	to move	力	strength
物	wù	thing	牛	ox

一 广 产 乐 乐 乐 乐 乐

乐 乐 乐 霁 需 需

、 丷 宀 宀 宔 实 实 **實**

丿 亻 仁 什 仕 世 借 借 借

、 亠 广 广 庀 应 应　　**應**

一 コ 尸 尸 尸 尸 尸 屋

屋 属 属 属

丿 八 少 父 爷 爷 爸 爸

丿 卜 仁 牛

一 二 云 云 云 动　　**動**

丿 卜 牛 牛 半 牣 物 物

鼠	shǔ	rat	鼠		rat
虎	hǔ	tiger	虍		tiger
兔	tù	rabbit	儿		son
龙	lóng	dragon	龙		dragon
蛇	shé	snake	虫		insect
羊	yáng	sheep	羊		sheep
猴	hóu	monkey	犭		animal
鸡	jī	chicken	鸟		bird
狗	gǒu	dog	犭		animal

ˊ 厂 戶 臼 臼 臼 臼 臼

臼 鼠 鼠 鼠 鼠

丨 ⺊ 卢 卢 庐 虍 虏 虎

ノ ⺈ ⺈ 夕 夕 色 争 免 兔

一 ナ 尤 龙 龙　　　龍

丨 冂 口 中 虫 虫 虫 虫

蚊 蚊 蛇

丶 丷 兰 兰 兰 羊

ノ ノ 犭 犭 犭 犭 犷 犷

犷 犷 猴 猴 猴

フ ㄨ ㄨ 鸡 鸡 鸡 鸡　　雞

ノ ノ 犭 犭 狗 狗 狗 狗

48 Forty-eighth Lesson

号	hào	number	口		mouth
星	xīng	star	日		sun
期	qī	period (*length of time*)	月		moon
加	jiā	to add	力		strength
坡	pō	slope	土		earth
嗯	ng	hm! (*exclam.*)	口		mouth
准	zhǔn	correct	冫		ice
分	fēn	minute	刀		knife
钟	zhōng	clock, bell	钅		metal

丨 冂 口 吕 号 　号

丨 冂 冃 冃 日 尸 尸 昌 畢 星

一 十 卄 卄 甘 甘 其 其 其

期 期 期 期

丿 力 加 加 加

一 十 土 圹 圹 圹 坡 坡

丨 冂 冃 叫 叫 叫 叫 叫 叫

咽 咽 嗯 嗯 嗯

丶 冫 冫 冫 汁 汁 汁 汁 准

准 准 　準

丿 八 分 分

丿 丿 二 乍 乍 钅 钅 钅 钟 鐘

急	jí	hurried	心		heart
糊	hú		米		rice
涂	tú	confused	氵		water
备	bèi	to prepare	田		field
堆	duī	pile	土		earth
送	sòng	to give (a gift)	辶		walk
恐	kǒng	to fear	心		heart
超	chāo	to overtake	走		walk

′ ⺈ ⼓ 刍 刍 刍 急 急 急

丶 丷 丷 半 半 米 籵 籵

籵 粁 粘 糊 糊 糊 糊

丶 冫 冫 氵 氵 氵 冷 泠 泠

泠 涂　　　　　　　塗

′ ⼓ 夂 冬 各 各 备 备　備

一 十 土 圤 圤 圤 坼 坼

坼 堆 堆

丶 丷 丷 丷 羊 关 关 送 送

一 丆 工 卫 巩 巩 巩 恐 恐 恐

一 十 土 キ キ 走 走 起

起 起 超 超

| 重 | zhòng | heavy | 日 | sun |
| 又 | yòu | once again | 又 | once again |

Note. Certain Chinese characters have two pronunciations with two different meanings. 重 can be read zhòng and mean *heavy*.

51　Fifty-first Lesson

从	cóng	from	人	person
图	tú	plan, drawing	囗	surrounding wall
干	gàn	to do	干	to do
嘛	má	(*particle*)	口	mouth
词	cí	word	讠	word
典	diǎn	register	八	eight

Note. The character 干 gàn can be read in two ways: gàn (*to do*) and gān (*dry*).

一 二 亍 育 育 言 亘 重 重 重

刁 又

It can also be read **chóng** and mean *again* (see **chóng** lesson 32).
Remember to make the distinction between the two pronunciations
according to the context.

丿 丬 丛 从　　　　　　　　**從**

丨 冂 冂 図 図 图 图 图　　**圖**

一 二 干　　　　　　　　　**幹**

丨 冂 巾 口 口ˋ 吁 旷 旷 旷 昕

庍 麻 庨 嘛 嘛 嘛

丶 讠 订 讨 词 词 词

丨 冂 曰 由 曲 曲 典 典

These two characters have been simplified. The old versions are
very different (see lesson 93).

科	kē	science	禾		cereal
技	jì	technique	扌		hand
版	bǎn	to publish	片		slice
而	ér	and	而		and
且	qiě	however	一		one
印	yìn	to print	阝		ear
万	wàn	ten thousand	一		one
咱	zán	us, we	口		mouth

52 Fifty-second Lesson

| 视 | shì | vision | 礻 | | rites |
| 趣 | qù | interest | 走 | | walk |

科

技

版

而

且

印

一 丆 万　萬

咱　嗒

視

走

趣

木	mù	wood	木		wood
偶	ǒu	statuette	亻		person
相	xiàng	to observe	目		eye
声	shēng	sound	士		scholar
周	Zhōu	(name)	口		mouth
更	gèng	more	曰		speak
节	jié	festival	艹		grass
目	mù	eye	目		eye
首	shǒu	head	首		head
但	dàn	but	亻		person
哎	āi	hey! (*exclam.*)	口		mouth

一 十 才 木
丿 亻 亻 伊 伊 伊 伊 偶
偶 偶 偶
一 十 才 木 朾 机 相 相 相
一 十 吉 吉 吉 吉 声　聲
丿 冂 月 冃 丹 周 周 周
一 丆 万 丏 亘 更 更
一 十 艹 节 节　　節
丨 冂 月 月 目
丶 丷 艹 艹 产 首 首 首
丿 亻 亻 们 伯 伯 但
丨 冂 口 叮 叮 哎 哎 哎

侯	Hóu	(name)	亻	person

林	lín	forest	木	wood
郭	Guō	(name)	阝	ear
启	qǐ	to initiate	户	family
儒	rú	scholar, disciple	亻	person

Note. Be careful not to confuse the family name 侯 hòu with 候 hóu in 时候 shíhou (*moment*).

---

53 Fifty-third Lesson

辉	huī	brilliant	车	vehicle
名	míng	given name	口	mouth

丿 亻 仁 仁 仔 仔 侯 侯
侯 侯

一 十 才 木 木 村 材 林

丶 亠 广 古 亩 亨 享 享 郭 郭

丶 宀 彐 户 户 启 启

丿 亻 仁 仁 仁 侢 侢 侢
侢 侢 侢 侢 侢 儒 儒 儒

In the name there is no short vertical stroke to the right of the *person* radical.

丨 丬 业 业 半 光 光 光

光 光 辉 辉 | 輝

丿 ク タ 夕 名 名

乡	xiāng	countryside		幺		fine thread
孙	sūn	grandson		子		child

54 Fifty-fourth Lesson

华	huá	China, brilliant		十		ten
侨	qiáo	to live abroad		亻		person
差	chà	to lack		工		work
每	měi	each		母		mother
锅	guō	pan		钅		metal
贴	tiē	to stick		贝		shell, cowrie
蒸	zhēng	to steam		灬		fire

㇉ 幺 乡　　　　　　　鄉

㇇ 了 孑 孖 孙 孙　　　　孫

丿 亻 仁 化 化 华　　　　華

丿 亻 仁 仁 伊 伕 侨 侨　　僑

丶 䒑 兰 兰 羊 羊 羊 差

丿 ㇐ 亡 勾 每 每 每

丿 ㇏ ㇄ ㇄ 钅 钅 钉 钌

钌 铝 锅 锅　　　　　　　鍋

丨 冂 贝 贝 则 㣇 贴 贴 贴 贴　貼

一 十 艹 艹 芗 芽 茅 莁

蒸 蒸 蒸 蒸 蒸

心	xīn	heart	心	heart
兄	xiōng	brother	儿	son
拿	ná	to take	手	hand
及	jí	to reach	丿	curve
检	jiǎn	to examine	木	wood
查	chá	to examine	木	wood
皮	pí	skin	皮	skin
箱	xiāng	trunk, box	⺮	bamboo
危	wēi	dangerous	卩	seal

丶 心 心 心

丨 冂 口 尸 兄

丿 人 𠆢 𠆢 合 合 合 倉

倉 拿

丿 𠃌 乃 及

一 十 才 木 朾 朾 柃 柃

柃 检 检   檢

一 十 才 木 杰 杏 杏 杳 查

一 厂 广 皮 皮

丿 𠂉 𥫗 𥫗 𥫗 竻 竻 竻

竻 笣 笴 箱 箱 箱 箱

丿 𠂊 𠂊 广 夗 危

险	xiǎn	difficult	阝	ear
偷	tōu	to steal	亻	person
注	zhù	to register, to record	氵	water
护	hù	to protect	扌	hand
照	zhào	to reflect	灬	fire
赶	gǎn	to catch up	走	walk

Note. Modern scripts (simplified characters) no longer make the distinction between what is now often called "right ear" 阝 and "left ear" 阝.

３ 阝 阝 阝 阶 险 险 险 险 **險**

／ 亻 亻 价 价 价 偷 偷 偷 偷 偷

丶 丶 氵 氵 汇 汇 汪 注

一 ナ 扌 扩 扩 护 护 **護**

｜ 冂 日 日 日 昭 昭 昭 昭 昭 照 照 照

一 十 土 丰 丰 走 走 走 走 赶 **趕**

In fact, 阝 placed on the left of a character is the simplification of the radical 阜 (*mound*). As for 阝 on the right side of a character, it is the simplification of the radical 邑 (*town*).

57 Fifty-seventh Lesson

些	xiē	some	二		two
楼	lóu	storey	木		wood
梦	mèng	dream	夕		eve
篇	piān	(*classifier*)	⺮		bamboo
鲁	lǔ	(name)	鱼		fish
迅	xùn	rapid	辶		walk
品	pǐn	products	口		mouth
赵	Zhào	(name)	走		walk

丨 卜 止 止 此 此 些 些

一 十 才 木 术 杧 杧 杧

杧 桝 楼 楼 楼　　　　　樓

一 十 才 木 木 村 材 林

梦 梦 梦　　　　　　　　夢

丿 广 竺 竹 竹 竹 竹 竹

竺 笁 笁 笆 笆 篇 篇

丿 仃 仃 仿 仿 鱼 鱼 鱼

鲁 鲁 鲁 鲁

乁 凡 凡 凡 讯 迅

丨 冂 口 吕 吕 品 品 品

一 十 土 キ キ 走 走 赵 赵 趙

树	shù	tree	木	tree
理	lǐ	reason	王	king

58 Fifty-eighth Lesson

戴	dài	to wear	戈	spear
眼	yǎn	eye	目	eye
镜	jìng	lens, spectacles	钅	metal
简	jiǎn	simple	⺮	bamboo

一 十 十 才 木 朳 权 杖 树 树

樹

一 二 干 王 王 丮 玌 玌 珇 珇 理 理

一 十 土 产 吉 吉 青 壴

壴 車 壴 壴 壴 壴 戠 戴 戴

丨 刂 刀 月 目 目 目 目

眼 眼 眼

丿 丆 乍 乍 乍 钅 钅 钅

钅 钅 钅 镜 镜 镜 镜 镜 鏡

丿 广 片 片 竹 竹 竹 竿

竹 竹 筒 简 简

簡

德	dé	virtue	彳	walk
运	yùn	transport	辶	walk
气	qì	breath	气	gas
母	mǔ	mother	母	mother

59 Fifty-ninth Lesson

往	wǎng	towards	彳	walk
拐	guǎi	to turn	扌	hand
山	shān	mountain	山	mountain
街	jiē	street	彳	walk
平	píng	flat	一	one

丿 彳 彳 彳 彳 彳 彳 彳
彳 彳 徝 徝 徳 德 德
一 二 テ 云 云 运 运　運
丿 仁 仨 气　　　　　氣
乚 囗 凸 母 母

丿 彳 彳 彳 彳 彳 往 往
一 十 扌 扌 护 护 拐 拐
丨 屮 山
丿 彳 彳 彳 彳 彳 往 往
徎 街 街 街
一 亠 亚 平 平

直	zhí	straight	十	ten
租	zū	to rent	禾	cereal
着	zhe, zháo	(*suffix*)	目	eye

玩	wán	to play	王	king
笑	xiào	to laugh	⺮	bamboo
挺	tǐng	very	扌	hand

Note. The suffix 着 indicating a continuous action is pronounced **zhe**. When this character is used in a verb compound to indicate the success of an action, it is pronounced **zháo**.

---

60   Sixtieth Lesson

| 酒 | jiǔ | alcohol | 氵 | water |

| 井 | jǐng | well (noun) | 二 | two |

一 ナ 广 古 古 首 直 直

一 二 千 禾 利 和 和 租

丶 丷 쓰 쓰 쓰 羊 养 着

着 着

一 二 千 王 玗 玗 玩 玩

ノ ケ ケ 竺 竺 竺 竺 笑 笑

一 十 扌 扩 扩 折 挺 挺 挺

酒 酒 酒

一 二 井 井

| 绿 | lù | green | 纟 | silk |

| 茉 | mò | | ++ | grass |
| 莉 | lì | } jasmine | ++ | grass |

| 糖 | táng | sugar | 米 | rice |

| 般 | bān | sort | 舟 | ship |

茅	máo	reed	++	grass
台	tái	platform	口	mouth
倒	dào	on the contrary	亻	person

乙 纟 纟 纠 纠 纠 纠 绿
绿 绿 绿　　　　　　绿

一 十 艹 芒 芒 芊 芊 茉
一 十 艹 芒 芒 芊 芋 莉
莉 莉

丶 丷 丷 半 半 米 米 粒
粒 粒 粒 粒 糖 糖 糖 糖

丿 丆 刀 刀 舟 舟 舟 舨
舨 般

一 十 艹 芌 芋 芋 芧 茅

乙 厶 台 台 台

丿 亻 亻 亻 侄 侄 侄 侄 倒 倒

| 谓 | wèi | to call | 讠 | word |
| 醉 | zuì | drunk | 酉 | container |

61 Sixty-first Lesson

使	shǐ	to cause, to enable	亻	person
转	zhuǎn	to change	车	vehicle
遍	biàn	time	辶	walk

Note. You can recognize the element on the right in 转 which is the phonetic indication. This is 专 which in isolation is pronounced zhuǎn.

丶 讠 讠 讵 讵 谓 谓 谓
谓 谓 谓   謂

一 厂 厂 厇 西 西 酉 酉丶
酉 酉一 酉丶 醉 醉 醉 醉

ノ 亻 仁 仁 佢 佢 使 使
一 七 车 车 车 车 轩 转 转
                        轉

丶 亠 亠 户 户 肩 肩 扁
扁 扁 遍 遍

Similarly in 遍, you can recognize 扁, the phonetic element. It is also found in the classifier 篇 (lesson 57), and sounds similar, as it is pronounced piān.

62 Sixty-second Lesson

附	fù	to add	阝	ear
婆	pó	old woman	女	woman
豆	dòu	bean, soya	豆	bean, soya
腐	fǔ	to coagulate	肉	meat
辣	là	hot, spicy	辛	bitter
馄	hún	\begin{tabular} dumpling \end{tabular}	饣	food
饨	dun		饣	food
骨	gǔ	bone	骨	bone

Note. For 腐 there is an unofficial simplification: 付.

阝 阝 阝 阝 阵 附 附

丶 丶 氵 氵 沪 沪 波 波 波 婆 婆

一 丆 丆 豆 豆 豆 豆

丶 亠 广 广 广 庐 庐 府

庐 庐 腐 腐 腐 腐

丶 亠 丶 亠 立 立 辛 辛

辛 辛 辛 辣 辣 辣

丿 𠂆 饣 饣 饣 饣 饣 饣

馄 馄 馄　　　　　　饂

丿 𠂆 饣 饣 饣 饣 饨　　　饂

丨 冂 冃 冎 冎 丹 骨 骨

骨 骨

64   Sixty-fourth Lesson

古	gǔ	ancient	口	mouth
留	líu	to leave, to remain	田	field
康	kāng	health	广	shelter
将	jiāng	in future	寸	thumb
义	yì	justice, right	丶	dot
游	yóu	to travel	氵	water
			丶	
浒	hǔ	bank	氵	water

Note. For 留 there is an unofficial simplification which is 㽞.

一 十 十 古 古

丶 乙 ㄅ 幻 幼 㿼 留 留 留

丶 宀 广 庐 庐 庐 庚 庚
庚 庚 康

丶 冫 丬 丬 㳿 㳿 㳿 㳿 将 将

丿 乂 义

丶 丶 氵 氵 汸 汸 汸 游
游 游 游 游

丶 丶 氵 氵 汸 汸 汸 汸 汸 淅

| 传 | zhuàn | narrative, biography | 亻 | person |
| 津 | jīn | ford | 氵 | water |

65 Sixty-fifth Lesson

柴	chái	firewood	木	wood
支	zhī	(*classifier*)	十	ten
圆	yuán	round	口	surrounding wall
珠	zhū	pearl	王	king (jade)
民	mín	people	氏	clan
光	guāng	light	儿	son

Note. The radical *king* 王 wáng is now usually also considered to be the radical for *jade*, 玉 yù, but according to the character, *jade*

丿 亻 仁 仁 传 传 传　　**傳**

丶 丶 氵 沪 沪 沪 津 津 津

丨 ⊢ 止 止 此 此 些 柴

柴 柴

一 十 支 支

丨 冂 冂 冂 冂 冃 同 圆

圆 圆　　　　　　　**圓**

一 二 王 王 玎 珒 玤 珠 珠

乛 ⁊ 尸 尸 民

丶 丷 丷 半 兴 光

may appear to be in the position of radical.
Be careful: do not confuse 光 guāng and 兴 xìng.

| 播 | bō | to spread, to transmit | 扌 | hand |

66 Sixty-sixth Lesson

| 咖 | kā | } coffee | 口 | mouth |
| 啡 | fēi | | 口 | mouth |

| 头 | tóu | head | 大 | big |
| 躺 | tǎng | to lie down | 身 | body |

| 床 | chuáng | bed | 广 | shelter |

67 Sixty-seventh Lesson

| 风 | fēng | wind | 风 | wind |

一 十 扌 扩 扩 扩 护 护
护 採 採 播 播 播 播

丨 冂 日 叮 叻 咖 咖 咖
丨 冂 日 叫 叶 吋 吋 �
啡 啡 啡

丶 丷 ニ 头 头　　　　　頭

丿 亻 勹 勺 身 身 身' 身"
身" 身" 躬 躺 躺 躺 躺

丶 亠 广 广 庀 床 床

丿 几 凡 风　　　　　風

哇	wa	(*exclam.*)	口		mouth
划	huá	to row	刂		knife
船	chuán	boat	舟		boat
泳	yǒng	to swim	氵		water
熊	xióng	bear	灬		fire

---

68 Sixty-eighth Lesson

故	gù	ancient	攵		letters
宫	gōng	palace	宀		roof
颐	yí	harmony	页		leaf

Note. Pay attention to the left part of 颐. It is 匝 and not 臣 !

丨 冂 口 旷 吐 哇 哇 哇 哇

一 七 戈 戈 戋 划 劃

′ 厂 ⺉ 舟 舟 舟 舫 舫

舩 船 船

丶 丶 氵 氵 汀 汩 泳 泳

厶 厶 合 台 台 育 能 能

能 能 能 能 熊 熊

一 十 士 古 古 故 故 故 故

丶 丷 宀 宀 宁 宁 宫 宫

一 厂 厂 厂 臣 臣 臣 臣

臣 臣 颐 颐 颐 颐 颐 頤

陵	líng	tomb	阝	ear (mound)
逛	guàng	to stroll	辶	walk
寄	jì	to send	宀	roof
唉	ēi	(exclam.)	口	mouth

---

69 Sixty-ninth Lesson

或	huò	or	戈	spear
湾	wān	gulf	氵	water

了 阝 阝⁻ 阝⁺ 阡 阡 陟 陟
陟 陵

丿 彡 犭 犭 犭 狂 狂
逛 逛

丶 宀 宀 宊 宊 宊 宊
宊 寄 寄

丨 冂 冎 咹 咹 咹 咹 咹
唉 唉

一 丆 丆 戓 戓 或 或 或

丶 丶 氵 氵 汇 汴 汴 泞
泞 湾 湾 湾

灣

之	zhī	(*particle*)	丶		dot
叔	shū	uncle	又		again
阿	ā	(*prefix*)	阝		ear
姨	yí	aunt	女		woman
爷	yé	grandfather	父		paternal

71 Seventy-first Lesson

副	fù	secondary	刂		blade
程	chéng	process	禾		cereal
计	jì	to count	讠		word

Note. Pay attention to memorizing the characters! Of the ten fù introduced in this book, there are seven which are fourth tone: fù.

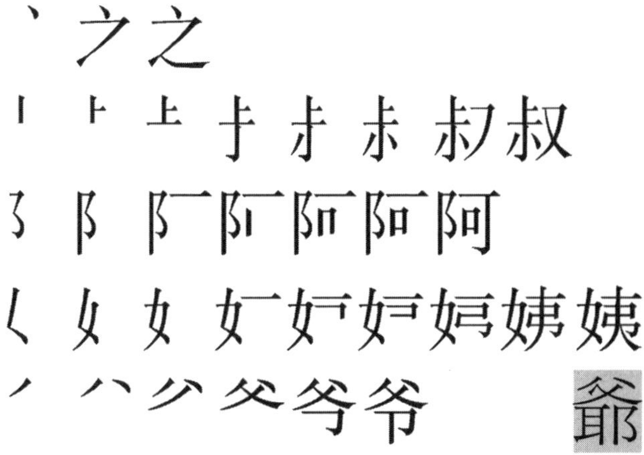

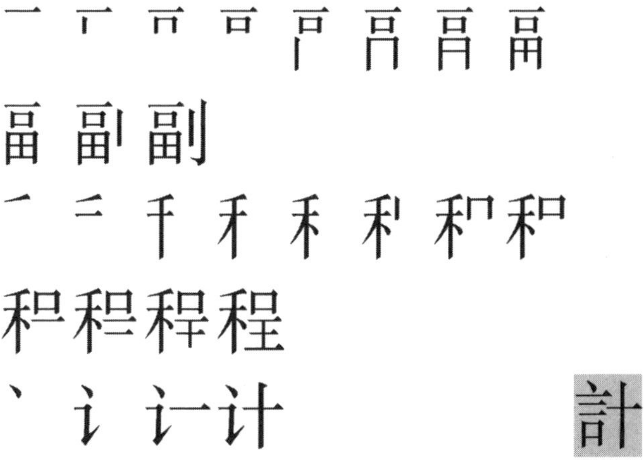

A quick glance through the index will help you to distinguish between the various characters with the same pronunciation.

委	wěi	delegate	女	woman
讨	tǎo		讠	word
论	lùn	} to discuss	讠	word

72 Seventy-second Lesson

继	jì		纟	silk
		} to continue		
续	xù		纟	silk

| 资 | zī | riches | 贝 | shell, cowrie |

| 便 | pián | cheap | 亻 | person |

Note. Once again, here is a character that can be pronounced in two different ways with two different meanings.

一 二 千 禾 禾 委 委 委

丶 讠 讠 讨 讨　　　討

丶 讠 讠 讨 讨 论 论　　論

乚 乡 乡 乡 纟 纟 纟 纟 纟 纟

纟 继　　　繼

乚 乡 乡 纟 纟 纟 纟 纟 纟

纟 纟 续　　　續

丶 冫 冫 冫 冫 次 次 咨

咨 资　　　資

丿 亻 亻 仁 仃 俏 俏 便 便

便 can be read as biàn, *easy*, or pián, according to context.

73   Seventy-third Lesson

室	shì	hall	宀	roof
美	měi	beautiful	羊	sheep
派	pài	to send	氵	water

74   Seventy-fourth Lesson

条	tiáo	(*classifier*)	木	wood
页	yè	leaf	页	leaf
行	háng	branch	彳	walk
建	jiàn	to build	廴	walk
议	yì	proposition	讠	word
至	zhì	to attain	至	arrive

Advice. Pay attention to the *walk* radical in 建, which is a variant of 辶. There is no initial dot: 廴.
For 建 the simplification 迠 is sometimes used.

、 丶 宀 宀 宀 宏 空 室 室

、 ⺌ 业 兰 羊 羊 羊 美 美

、 丶 氵 氵 沪 沪 沪 派 派 派

ク 夂 冬 条 条 条

一 丆 厂 兯 页 页 頁

丿 ㇆ 彳 彳 行 行

フ ㇇ ㇋ 彐 彐 聿 建 建

、 讠 讠 议 议 議

一 云 厷 至 至 至

Note. Here is a new character that has two pronunciations: 行, can be read xíng or háng according to the meaning and the context.

须	xū	must, to have to	页	leaf
领	lǐng	to lead	页	leaf
导	dǎo	to guide	寸	thumb
示	shì	to indicate	示	show
答	dá	answer	⺮	bamboo

75　Seventy-fifth Lesson

团	tuán	group	囗	surrounding wall
务	wù	task	力	strength
赞	zàn	to assist	贝	shell, cowrie

丿 丿丿 彡 彳 纩 彳 须 须 须 **須**

丿 丿 八 乆 今 令 令 令 钌

领 领 领   **領**

一 コ ㅌ 异 导 导   **導**

一 二 于 亣 示

丿 亇 大 癶 竺 竺 竺 笑

笁 竺 答 答

丨 冂 冃 丹 团 团   **團**

丿 夕 夕 务 务   **務**

丿 仁 牛 生 步 先 先 兂

兟 兟 梦 梵 兟 赞 赞 **贊**

流	líu	to flow	氵	water
利	lì	interest	刂	blade
随	suí	according to	阝	ear
谦	qiān	modest	讠	word
虚	xū		虍	tiger
发	fā	pronunciation	又	again
音	yīn		日	sun

丶 丶 氵 氵 氵 氵 氵 氵
泸 流
一 二 千 禾 禾 和 利
了 阝 阝 阝 阝 阝 阝 阝 阝
陌 随 随 随　　　　　随
丶 讠 讠 讠 讠 讠 讠 讠
讲 讲 谦 谦
丨 ㇠ 声 卢 卢 虎 虎 虎
虎 虚 虚
丶 一 ナ 步 发 发　　发
丶 亠 亠 立 音 音 音
音 音

76   Seventy-sixth Lesson

访	fǎng	to visit	讠	word
招	zhāo	to call, to hail	扌	hand
待	dài	to treat	彳	walk
考	kǎo	exam	耂	old
纪	jì	to note	纟	silk
双	shuāng	double	又	again
签	qiān	to sign	𥫗	bamboo
离	lí	distant	禸	track
任	rèn	to appoint	亻	person

、　讠　订　讧　访　访　　　訪

一　寸　扌　扩　护　护　招　招

丿　彳　彳　彳　彳　往　往　待　待

一　十　土　耂　考　考

乚　纟　纟　纟　纪　纪　纪　　　紀

フ　又　双　双　　　雙

丿　⺮　⺮　⺮　⺮　笶　笶　笶

笶　笶　答　签　签　　　簽

、　亠　䒑　文　𠆢　卤　㐫　离

离　离　　　離

丿　亻　仁　仁　任　任

78 Seventy-eighth Lesson

扎	zhā	to pierce	扌		hand
针	zhēn	needle	钅		metal
疼	téng	to suffer	疒		illness
灸	jiǔ	to cauterize	火		fire
效	xiào	efficiency	攵		letters
试	shì	to try	讠		word
伯	bó	uncle	亻		person
医	yī	medicine	匚		basket
于	yú	at	一		one

Note. 针灸 means *acupuncture and moxibustion.*

一 寸 扌 扎

丿 𠂉 𠂉 𠂉 钅 钅 针

丶 亠 广 广 疒 疒 疒 疼
疼 疼

丿 夕 夕 冬 冬 灸 灸

丶 亠 广 六 � 交 効 効
効 效

丶 讠 讠 讠 讠 讠 试 试 試

丿 亻 亻 亻 伯 伯 伯

一 匚 匸 匚 医 医 医 醫

一 二 于 於

The term 扎针 refers only to acupuncture using fine needles inserted through the skin at various points on the body to anesthetize, treat or relieve pain.

79　Seventy-ninth Lesson

传	chuán	to transmit	亻	person
盘	pán	game, tray	皿	vessel
手	shǒu	hand	手	hand
件	jiàn	correspondence	亻	person
载	zǎi	to load	戈	axe

80　Eightieth Lesson

冬	dōng	winter	冫	ice
度	dù	degree	广	shelter
受	shòu	to submit, to suffer	爫	claw
了	liǎo	finish	亅	hook
夏	xià	summer	夂	follow

丿 亻 仁 仨 传 传

丿 丿 丿 内 舟 舟 舟 舟

舟 盘 盘 盤

一 二 三 手

丿 亻 亻 仁 仨 件

一 十 丰 寺 去 弄 车 轧 载 载

丿 夕 夂 冬 冬

丶 亠 广 广 庐 庐 庐 庐 度 度

一 亠 亠 亠 严 严 受 受

乛 了

一 一 厂 厂 百 百 百 頁 夏 夏

闷	mēn	stuffy	心	heart
潮	cháo	damp	氵	water
湿	shī	damp	氵	water
秋	qīu	autumn	禾	cereal

Note. Do not confuse the *follow* radical 夂 and the *strike* radical 攵. The former has three strokes, the third stroke starting at the base of the first stroke. The latter has four strokes, the third starting under the second stroke. This radical is called *letters* because it is a variant of the character 文 wén (*language, letters*). Not to be confused with the *woman* radical: 女 nǚ!

---

81 Eighty-first Lesson

| 棋 | qí | chess, Go | 木 | wood |

丶 冂 冂 冂 冋 冋 冋 **悶**

丶 丶 氵 氵 氵 氵 沽 沽
沽 渣 淖 潮 潮 潮 潮

丶 丶 氵 氵 沪 沪 沪 沪
浬 湿 湿 湿 **濕**

一 二 千 千 禾 禾 禾 秋 秋

Note. Some characters are very evocative: 悶 is the *heart* 心 enclosed by *doors* 门 mén. In *autumn* 秋, the crops are the color of *fire* 火 huǒ.

一 十 才 木 杧 杧 杧 柑
柑 柑 棋 棋 **棋**

围	wéi	to encircle	囗	surrounding wall
耐	nài	to endure, to bear	寸	inch
性	xìng	character, nature	忄	heart

82 Eighty-second Lesson

| 航 | háng | to navigate | 舟 | boat |
| 量 | liàng | quantity | 曰 | to say |

Note. You should distinguish 日 *sun* (or *day*) from 曰 *to say*, which is wider and flatter.

83 Eighty-third Lesson

邻	lín	neighborhood	阝	ear
居	jū	to live, to dwell	尸	corpse
交	jiāo	exchange	亠	lid

丨 冂 冂 冃 同 凬 围 　围

一 厂 厂 丆 而 而 　耐 耐 耐

丨 忄 忄 忄 忄 忙 　性 性

丶 丆 力 刀 舟 舟 舟 舟

舟 航

丨 冂 冂 日 旦 昌 昌 昌

昌 量 量 量

丿 𠂉 𠂉 今 令 令 邻 　鄰

乛 コ 尸 尸 尸 尸 居 居

丶 亠 六 六 交 交

部	bù	ministry	阝	ear
整	zhěng	entire	止	stop
呗	bei	(*exclam.*)	口	mouth
希	xī	to hope	巾	cloth
望	wàng	to wish, to desire	月	flesh

Note. For 部 there is an unofficial simplification: 卩.

---

85 Eighty-fifth Lesson

停	tíng	to stop	亻	person

丶 亠 产 立 产 音 音

部 部

一 厂 厅 戸 审 東 束 束

敕 敕 敕 敕 敕 整 整 整

丨 冂 冃 冂 叨 呗 呗 唄

丿 乂 孚 乒 希 希 希

丶 亠 亡 讠 切 讱 讱 朢

朢 朢 望

丿 亻 亻 亻 广 广 停 停

停 停 停

86 Eighty-sixth Lesson

搬	bān	to move (house)	扌	hand
郊	jiāo	suburb	阝	ear
区	qū	quarter	匚	basket
院	yuàn	institute	阝	ear
石	shí	stone	石	stone
油	yóu	oil	氵	water
管	guǎn	to manage	⺮	bamboo

87 Eighty-seventh Lesson

银	yín	silver	钅	metal

一 十 扌 扩 扩 扚 扚 拐

拐 拐 拐 搬 搬

丶 亠 产 六 亥 交 交 郊

一 匚 匚 区 区　　　　　　區

乛 阝 阝 阝 阝 陌 陌 陌 陌 院

一 丆 石 石 石

丶 丶 氵 氵 沂 沏 油 油

丿 ⺮ ⺮ ⺮ 笁 笁 笁 笁

竺 竺 竺 管 管 管

丿 ⺊ ⺊ ⻐ 钅 钅 钅 钅

钊 钊 银　　　　　　　　銀

| 府 | fǔ | residence | 广 | | shelter |

88 Eighty-eighth Lesson

身	shēn	body	身	body
体	tǐ	body	亻	person
向	xiàng	towards	口	mouth
祝	zhù	to wish, to congratulate	礻	rites
乐	lè	joy	木	wood

89 Eighty-ninth Lesson

沟	gōu	ditch	氵	water
耳	ěr	ear	耳	ear
朵	duǒ	bud	木	wood
客	kè	guest	宀	roof

、 亠 广 广 广 庁 府 府

丶 亻 勹 勺 身 身 身

丿 亻 亻 仁 仕 付 休 体　體

丿 亻 门 门 向 向 向

丶 ス 才 衤 衤 衤 祁 祁 祝

一 厂 仁 乒 乐 乐　樂

、 丶 氵 氵 氵 汋 沟 沟　溝

一 丁 丌 开 耳 耳

丿 几 凸 朵 朵 朵　朵

丶 丷 宀 宀 灾 安 安 客 客

90 Ninetieth Lesson

| 除 | chú | apart from | 阝 | ear |
| 替 | tì | instead of, to replace | 日 | sun |

92 Ninety-second Lesson

| 迟 | chí | late, delay | 辶 | walk |
| 扰 | rǎo | to bother | 扌 | hand |

93 Ninety-third Lesson

杯	bēi	cup	木	wood
谊	yì	friendship	讠	word
健	jiàn	health	亻	person

了 阝 阝 阶 阶 阶 除 除 除
一 二 丰 丰 耒 耒 耔 耔
耔 替 替 替

一 コ 尸 尺 尺 迟 迟　遲
一 十 扌 扩 扐 扰 扰　擾

一 十 扌 木 杧 杯 杯 杯　盃
丶 讠 讠 讠 讠 讠 讠 谊
谊 谊　　　　　　　　　　誼
丿 亻 亻 亻 亻 亻 亻 律
律 健

顺	shùn	without obstacle	页	leaf
干	gān	dry	干	to do
功	gōng	success	力	strength

94 Ninety-fourth Lesson

其	qí	his, her, its, their	八	eight
忽	hū	suddenly	心	heart
窗	chuāng	window	穴	cave
户	hù	dwelling	户	dwelling
帮	bāng	to help	巾	cloth

Advice. Do not confuse 处 chù and 外 wài.
Do not confuse 户 hù and 尸 shī!

丿 丿 川 𠂢 𠂢 𠂢 順 順 順

順

乾

一 二 干

一 丁 工 巧 功

一 十 艹 艹 甘 甘 其 其 其

丿 勹 勹 勿 匆 忽 忽 忽

丶 宀 宀 穴 宓 宓 窏 穼

穼 窏 窗 窗

窓

丶 彐 彐 戶

一 ᆖ 三 聿 聿 邦 邦 帮 帮

幫

助	zhù	to help	力	strength
处	chù	place	夂	follow
丰	fēng	abundant	丨	vertical
富	fù	rich	宀	roof

---

96 Ninety-sixth Lesson

食	shí	food	食	food
堂	táng	hall	土	earth
影	yǐng	shadow	彡	fur
刻	kè	engrave, quarter (of an hour)	刂	blade

丨 刂 刂 刂 且 助 助

丿 ク 夂 処 処　　處

一 二 三 丰　　豊

丶 宀 宀 宀 宀 宫 宫
宫 宫 富 富

丿 人 人 今 今 含 食 食 食

丶 丷 丷 丷 尚 尚 尚
尚 堂 堂

丨 刂 刂 日 旦 旦 早 昻
昻 景 景 景 影 影 影

丶 亠 亠 亥 亥 亥 刻 刻

| 坏 | huài | bad | | 土 | earth |
| 修 | xiū | to repair | | 亻 | person |

97 Ninety-seventh Lesson

餐	cān	meal		食	food
短	duǎn	short		矢	arrow
冰	bīng	ice		冫	ice
棍	gùn	stick		木	wood
拾	shí	to pick up		扌	hand

Note. For 餐 there is an unofficial simplification: 歺

一 十 土 圡 坊 圢 坏 坏 坏 壞

丿 亻 亻 伫 伫 修 修 修 修

丷 ヒ 戸 歺 歺 歺ㄱ 歺ㄨ 歺ㄨ

癶 癶 癶 飱 飱 餐 餐 餐

丿 ㄥ ㅌ 午 矢 矢 知 知

知 知 短 短

丶 丷 冫 冫 冫 冰 冰

一 十 才 木 杧 杧 杧 杧

梍 棍 棍 棍

一 寸 扌 扩 护 护 拎 拾 拾

99 Ninety-ninth Lesson

祖	zǔ	ancestors	礻	rites
呵	hè	(*exclam.*)	口	mouth
显	xiǎn	to reveal	日	sun
轻	qīng	light	车	vehicle

100 Hundredth Lesson

悟	wù	revelation	忄	heart
衣	yī	clothing	衣	clothing
料	liào	materials	米	rice
凉	liáng	cool	冫	ice

丶 ラ オ ネ 礻 初 祖 祖 祖

丨 冂 日 旷 旷 叮 叮 呵

丨 冂 日 日 日 早 昂 显 显 顯

一 も 车 车 轩 轻 轻 轻 轻

輕

丨 忄 忄 忄 忄 忤 悟 悟 悟

悟 悟

丶 亠 ナ ナ 衣 衣

丶 丷 并 半 米 米 米 米 料

丶 丬 冫 冫 广 汸 泸 泸 凉

凉 凉

药	yào	medicine	艹	grass

治	zhì	to cure	氵	water
痛	tòng	to suffer	疒	illness

Note. There are two characters to express the idea of being in pain:
痛 tòng and 疼 téng (see lesson 78).

102 One hundred and second Lesson

步	bù	step	止	stop
兜	dōu	pocket	儿	son

103 One hundred and third Lesson

供	gōng	to provide, to install	亻	person
池	chí	reservoir	氵	water

一 十 艹 艻 艻 艻 茐 药 药

药

丶 丶 氵 汁 汁 汵 治 治

丶 亠 广 广 疒 疒 疒 疒

病 病 痈 痛

丨 上 止 止 步 步 步

丶 ㇀ ㇁ 白 白 白 白

白 臽 兜

丿 亻 亻 什 世 供 供 供

丶 丶 氵 汕 汕 池

阳	yáng	sun, male	阝	ear
济	jì	to assist	氵	water
设	shè	to establish	讠	word

104 One hundred and fourth Lesson

| 白 | bái | white | 白 | white |

✳ ✳ ✳

阝 阝 阡 阳 阳 阳　　陽

丶 冫 氵 氵 汀 沪 泲 济 济　済

丶 讠 讠 讱 设 设　　設

———————————————————

′ 亻 亻 白 白

* * *

Index Of Characters
Introduced in Volumes 1 and 2
of Chinese With Ease

The numbers correspond to the lesson where the character is introduced for the first time; either on its own or with another character or characters as a polysyllabic word.

When you refer to the lesson you will find the analysis and explanation of the character.

For the same transcription, the characters are in order of **tone**. Characters with the same tone are placed in order of the number of their **strokes**.

Words starting with the consonant sh come after those starting with the letter s. In the same way those starting with zh come after those starting with z and words starting with ch come after those starting with c.

For certain particles or grammar words, no translation is given. Their grammatical function is given in brackets.

Note

Words, 词 cí, in Chinese are mostly **polysyllabic**, in other words made up of several characters, 字 zì.

The **INDEX** below contains all the characters you have met. The meaning of a character may bear little relation to the sense of a polysyllabic word in which it appears. In order to memorize the characters, it may be useful to replace them in context and memorize them as part of a word. To do so, refer to the lessons indicated for each character.

A

B

C

D

E

F

G

K

| lǔ | 旅 | travel ....29 |
| lǜ | 绿 | green ....60 |

M

mā	妈	mummy, mother 36
má	麻	hemp, linen, sesame 39
má	嘛	what? isn't it? 51
mǎ	马	horse 18
ma	吗	(*interr.*) 1
mǎi	买	to buy 3
mài	卖	to sell 32
mǎn	满	full, to fill 43
màn	慢	slow, slowly 38
máng	忙	busy, occupied 30
māo	猫	cat 67
máo	毛	hair, fur, ten cents 44
máo	茅	thatch 60
mào	冒	to risk, to brave 45
me	么	(*interr.*) 2
méi	没	not (have) 5
měi	每	each 54
měi	美	beautiful, pretty 73
mèi	妹	(younger) sister 11
mēn	闷	stuffy, oppressive 80
mén	门	door 25
men	们	(*plural*) 11
měng	蒙	Mongolian 37

N

Q

SH

W

ZH

The Index includes the 800 characters introduced in the two volumes of *Chinese with Ease*. Used in combination they provide the 1,500 words and expressions you have studied.

Table of Radicals
with Their Meaning

The list underneath includes the 214 traditional radicals as defined in the dictionary compiled in the reign of the Emperor KANGXI in the XVIIth century. Classical and simplified forms are both presented.

Sometimes a radical can have several forms, depending on whether it appears on the left of the character, or on the right, or to the top, or at the bottom. The different variants of a same radical are given under the same number.

#	RADICAL	MEANING
1	ー	horizontal
2	｜	vertical
3	丶	dot
4	ノ	left curve
5	乙	celestial stem no.2
6	亅	vertical hook
7	二	two

8	亠	lid
9	人 亻	person
10	儿	son
11	入	enter
12	八	eight
13	冂	wilderness
14	冖	cover
15	冫	ice
16	几	table, several
17	凵	container
18	刀 刂	blade
19	力	strength
20	勹	embrace
21	匕	spoon
22	匚	basket
23	匸	box
24	十	ten
25	卜	divination
26	卩 㔾	seal, stamp

27	厂	cliff
28	厶	private
29	又	again
30	口	mouth
31	囗	surrounding wall
32	土　圵	earth
33	士	scholar
34	夂	walking slowly
35	夊	overtaking, follow
36	夕	evening
37	大	big
38	女	woman
39	子　孑	child, terrestrial branch no.1
40	宀	roof
41	寸	inch, thumb
42	小	small
43	尢　尣	broken or curved leg
44	尸	corpse
45	屮	sprout

46	山	mountain
47	巜 川	river
48	工	work
49	己	self
50	巾	fabric, napkin
51	干	dry
52	幺	small, young
53	广	shelter
54	廴	walk
55	廾	two hands (bottom of character)
56	弋	shooting
57	弓	bow
58	彐 彐 彑	pig head
59	彡	hair, feather
60	彳	step
61	心 忄 忄	heart
62	戈	axe
63	戶	family

64	手 扌	hand
65	支	branch
66	攴 攵	whip, strike, letters
67	文	language
68	斗	bushel
69	斤	pound
70	方	square
71	无 旡	negative
72	日	sun
73	曰	speak
74	月	moon
75	木	wood
76	欠	lack
77	止	stop
78	歹 歺	bad, inauspicious
79	殳	halberd
80	毋 (母)	not (mother)
81	比	compare
82	毛	hair, fur

83	氏	clan
84	气	gas
85	水 氵 氺	water
86	灬 火	fire
87	爫 爪	claw
88	父	father
89	爻	crossing two times
90	爿	bed
91	片	slice
92	牙	tooth
93	牛 牜	ox
94	犬 犭	dog
95	玄	black, dark
96	玉 王	jade
97	瓜	gourd
98	瓦	tile
99	甘	sweet
100	生	born

101	用	use
102	田	field
103	疋	bolt of cloth
104	疒	illness
105	癶	two hands above
106	白	white
107	皮	skin
108	皿	vessel
109	目	eye
110	矛	spear
111	矢	arrow
112	石	stone
113	示 礻	show, rites
114	禸	animal stamping the earth
115	禾	cereals
116	穴	cavern
117	立	standing
118	竹 ⺮	bamboo
119	米	rice

120	糸 纟	silk
121	缶	crock, vessel
122	网	net
123	羊	sheep
124	羽	feather
125	老	old
126	而	then
127	耒	plough
128	耳	ear
129	聿	brush
130	肉 月	meat, flesh
131	臣	minister
132	自	self
133	至	arrive
134	臼	mortar
135	舌	tongue
136	舛	lying side by side
137	舟	boat
138	艮	simple, honest

139	色	color
140	艸 艹	grass
141	虍	tiger
142	虫	insect
143	血	blood
144	行	walk
145	衣 衤	clothing
146	西	west
147	見 见	see
148	角	horn
149	言 讠	word
150	谷	valley
151	豆	bean
152	豕	pig
153	豸	animal
154	貝 贝	shell
155	赤	vermilion
156	走 赱	walk
157	𧾷 足	foot

158	身	body
159	車 车	vehicle
160	辛	bitter, celestial stem no.8
161	辰	morning, terrestrial branch no.10
162	辶	walk
163	阝	ear (on the right)
164	酉	wine jar, terrestrial branch no.10
165	釆	pluck, pick
166	里	hamlet
167	金 釒 钅	metal, gold
168	長 长 镸	long
169	門 门	door
170	阝	ear (on the left)
171	录	reaching, catching
172	隹	short tail bird
173	雨	rain
174	青 专	green, blue

175	非		not
176	面		face, noodles
177	革		leather
178	韋	韦	tanned leather
179	韭		chives
180	音		sound
181	頁	页	page
182	風	风	wind
183	飛	飞	fly
184	食	飠 饣	food
185	首		head
186	香		perfume
187	馬	马	horse
188	骨		bone
189	高		high
190	髟		hair
191	鬥		battle
192	鬯		offering spirits

193	鬲	vessel
194	鬼	spirit, ghost
195	魚 鱼	fish
196	鳥 鸟	bird
197	鹵	saltpeter
198	鹿	deer
199	麥 麦	wheat
200	麻	hemp
201	黃	yellow
202	黍	millet
203	黑	black
204	黹	needlework
205	黽 黾	frog
206	鼎	tripod
207	鼓	drum
208	鼠	rat
209	鼻	nose
210	齊 齐	gathering
211	齒 齿	tooth

212	龍　龙	dragon
213	龟	turtle
214	龠	flute

Bibliography

In English

VAN GULIK, Robert. *Chinese pictorial art*. New York: Hacker, 1981.

SCARPARI, Mauricio. "Origins and development of Chinese writing". *7000 years of Chinese civilization*. Milan: Silvana Editoriale, 1983.

GUO Bonan. *Gate to Chinese Calligraphy*. Beijing: Foreign Languages Press, 1995.

YIN Binhong. *Modern Chinese characters*. Beijing: Sinolingua, 1994.

KRAUS, Richard Kurt. *Brushes with power: Modern politics and the Chinese art of calligraphy*. Berkeley: California University Press, 1991.

MACNAUGHTON, William. *Reading and writing Chinese*: a guide to the Chinese writing system. Tokyo Japan and Rutland Vermont: Tuttle, 1997.

ZHOU Jian. *500 basic Chinese characters, a speedy elementary course*. Beijing: Sinolingua, 1996.

WENG Li. *Hutongs of Beijing*. Beijing: Beijing Arts and Photography, 1995.

SULLIVAN, M. *The arts of China*. Berkeley: California University Press, 1984.

TREGEAR, Mary. *Chinese Art*. London: Thames and Hudson, 1991.

In Chinese

Lᴉɴ Sili (Cecilia Lᴉɴᴅǫᴠɪsᴛ). 汉字王国 Hànzì wángguó.
Shandong: Shandong huabao chubanshe Publishing House, 1998.

An illustrated history of the development of the Chinese script,
showing examples of early writing and documented with photographs
of Chinese architecture and objects related to pictograms.

Aubin Imprimeur
LIGUGÉ, POITIERS

Achevé d'imprimer en janvier 2006
N° d'édition 2333 / N° d'impression P 69614
Dépôt légal, janvier 2006
Imprimé en France